FAVORITE BRAND NAME™

CHICKEN

Publications International, Ltd.
Favorite Brand Name Recipes at www.fbnr.com

Louis Weber, CEO
Publications International, Ltd.
7373 North Cicero Avenue
Lincolnwood, IL 60712

Some of the products listed in this publication may be in limited distribution.

Front cover photography by Chris Cassidy Photography, Inc.

Pictured on the front cover *(clockwise from top left):* Cobb Salad *(page 48),* Herb Roasted Chicken *(page 292),* Chicken Prosciutto Rolls *(page 328),* Chicken and Mozzarella Melts *(page 136)* and Chicken and Fruit Kabobs *(page 10).*
Pictured on the jacket flaps: Hula Chicken Salad with Orange Poppy Seed Dressing *(page 66)* and Chicken and Spicy Black Bean Tacos *(page 210).*
Pictured on the back cover *(clockwise from top):* Soy-Glazed Chicken Wings *(page 8),* Greek Chicken and Artichoke Rice *(page 318),* Middle Eastern Chicken Soup *(page 104)* and Chicken Couscous *(page 360).*

ISBN-13: 978-1-4127-1681-9
ISBN-10: 1-4127-1681-0

Library of Congress Control Number: 2008934877

Manufactured in China.

8 7 6 5 4 3 2 1

Microwave Cooking: Microwave ovens vary in wattage. Use the cooking times as guidelines and check for doneness before adding more time.

Preparation/Cooking Times: Preparation times are based on the approximate amount of time required to assemble the recipe before cooking, baking, chilling or serving. These times include preparation steps such as measuring, chopping and mixing. The fact that some preparations and cooking can be done simultaneously is taken into account. Preparation of optional ingredients and serving suggestions is not included.

CONTENTS

CHOOSING CHICKEN

What is lean, nutritious, easy to prepare and goes with everything? Chicken, of course! Whether you want a tasty snack or an elegant appetizer, a healthy salad or a hearty casserole, a showstopping supper or a quick weeknight meal, you'll find the perfect recipe in this collection. A quick trip to the supermarket is all it takes to see why savvy shoppers choose chicken when it's time to get cooking.

ON THE SHELVES

Chicken broth can serve as a base for soups and stews and add greater depth of flavor when cooking rice or beans. Look for organic, low-fat and reduced-sodium options that can be substituted in any recipe to tailor it to your nutritional and dietary goals.

Shelf-stable cooked chicken breast packed in water can be found in cans and pouches, making it a convenient pantry staple. Simply drain and add to pastas, casseroles, salads and quesadillas for a satisfying supper in minutes.

IN THE FREEZER

Buying frozen raw chicken saves time and money. For convenience, much of it is available pre-portioned into individually wrapped packages of one or two servings, allowing you to defrost only what you need for that meal. Commercially processed chicken is frozen much faster and more efficiently than chicken frozen after purchase, reducing the likelihood of freezer burn, and buying in bulk reduces grocery costs dramatically.

The selection of frozen precooked chicken products is growing steadily. Chicken wings, chicken nuggets, chicken patties, seasoned chicken breasts and more make preparing tasty snacks and meals as easy as turning on the oven.

IN THE MEAT SECTION

At any grocery store, large or small, you will find a broad range of fresh raw chicken products in the meat section. Choose from whole roasting chickens, petite Cornish hens, ground chicken and chicken parts, including wings, breasts, thighs, drumsticks and quarters. You'll also find convenient options like boneless skinless breasts, thighs and tenders, which make chicken leaner and even easier to prepare.

You will also find precooked chicken strips, deli chicken breast and ready-to-serve rotisserie-cooked whole chickens. Available simply roasted or cooked with a variety of seasonings, these are convenient options for putting dinner on the table in a hurry.

PLAYING IT SAFE

Food safety is critical when handling and preparing raw chicken. To avoid possible salmonella contamination, be sure to wash your hands, knives and work surfaces with hot soapy water after handling raw chicken. If possible, dedicate one cutting board to working with raw meats and a second for chopping produce. Otherwise, always work with raw chicken last to avoid any chance of contaminating the rest of your ingredients. If your cutting boards cannot go in the dishwasher, clean them regularly with a mild bleach solution to kill any bacteria that may have settled into scratches in the surface.

GLOBAL STARTERS

CHIPOTLE CHICKEN QUESADILLAS

- 1 package (8 ounces) cream cheese, softened
- 1 cup (4 ounces) shredded Mexican cheese blend
- 1 tablespoon minced chipotle pepper in adobo sauce
- 5 (10-inch) flour tortillas
- 5 cups shredded cooked chicken (about 1¼ pounds)
- Nonstick cooking spray
- Guacamole, sour cream, salsa and chopped fresh cilantro

1. Combine cream cheese, cheese blend and chipotle pepper in large bowl.

2. Spread ⅓ cup cheese mixture over half of one tortilla. Top with about 1 cup chicken. Fold over tortilla. Repeat with remaining tortillas.

3. Heat large nonstick skillet over medium-high heat. Spray outside surface of each tortilla with cooking spray. Cook 4 to 6 minutes or until lightly browned, turning once.

4. Cut into wedges. Serve with guacamole, sour cream, salsa and cilantro.

Makes 5 servings

Note: Chipotle peppers in adobo sauce can be found in small cans in the Mexican food section of the supermarket.

SOY–GLAZED CHICKEN WINGS

2 tablespoons dry sherry
2 tablespoons soy sauce
1 tablespoon sugar
1 tablespoon cornstarch
3 cloves garlic, minced, divided
1 teaspoon red pepper flakes
3 pounds chicken wings, tips removed and cut into halves
2 tablespoons vegetable oil
3 green onions, cut into 1-inch pieces
¼ cup chicken broth
1 teaspoon dark sesame oil
1 tablespoon toasted sesame seeds

1. For marinade, combine sherry, soy sauce, sugar, cornstarch, 2 cloves garlic and pepper flakes in large bowl; mix well. Stir in chicken wings; cover and marinate overnight in refrigerator, turning occasionally.

2. Drain wings, reserving marinade. Heat wok or large deep skillet over high heat 1 minute. Add vegetable oil and heat 30 seconds. Add half of wings; cook 10 to 15 minutes or until wings are brown on all sides, turning occasionally. Remove with slotted spoon to another large bowl; set aside. Reheat oil in wok 30 seconds and repeat with remaining wings. Reduce heat to medium. Drain off any remaining oil.

3. Add remaining clove garlic and green onions to wok; cook and stir 30 seconds. Add wings and broth. Cover and cook 5 minutes or until wings are cooked through, stirring occasionally.

4. Add reserved marinade; bring to a boil. Cook and stir 2 minutes or until wings are glazed with marinade. Add sesame oil; mix well. Transfer to serving platter; sprinkle with sesame seeds. Serve immediately.

Makes 6 to 8 servings

CHICKEN AND FRUIT KABOBS

- 1¾ cups honey
- ¾ cup fresh lemon juice
- ½ cup Dijon mustard
- ⅓ cup chopped fresh ginger
- 4 pounds boneless skinless chicken breasts, cut into 1-inch pieces
- 6 plums, pitted and quartered
- 4 cups pineapple chunks (about half of medium pineapple)

1. Prepare grill for direct cooking. Combine honey, lemon juice, mustard and ginger in small bowl; mix well. Alternately thread chicken and fruit onto skewers; brush generously with honey mixture.

2. Grill kabobs 15 to 20 minutes or until chicken is cooked through, turning and brushing frequently with honey mixture. *Do not baste during last 5 minutes.*

Makes 12 servings

CAJUN–STYLE CHICKEN NUGGETS

- 1 envelope LIPTON® RECIPE SECRETS® Onion Soup Mix*
- ½ cup plain dry bread crumbs
- 1½ teaspoons chili powder
- 1 teaspoon ground cumin
- 1 teaspoon dried thyme leaves, crushed (optional)
- ¼ teaspoon ground red pepper
- 2 pounds boneless chicken breasts, cut into 1-inch pieces
- BERTOLLI® Extra Light Olive Oil
- Assorted mustards (optional)

**Also terrific with LIPTON® RECIPE SECRETS® Onion Mushroom Soup Mix.*

1. In large bowl, combine soup mix, bread crumbs, chili powder, cumin, thyme and pepper. Dip chicken in bread crumb mixture, coating well.

2. In 12-inch skillet, heat ½ inch olive oil and cook chicken over medium heat, turning once, until thoroughly cooked; drain on paper towels. Serve warm and, if desired, with assorted mustards.

Makes about 5 dozen nuggets

TIPSY CHICKEN WRAPS

- 1 tablespoon dark sesame oil
- 1 pound ground chicken
- 8 ounces firm tofu, diced
- ½ red bell pepper, diced
- 3 green onions, sliced
- 1 tablespoon minced fresh ginger
- 2 cloves garlic, minced
- ½ cup Asian beer
- ⅓ cup hoisin sauce
- 1 teaspoon Asian chili sauce*
- ½ cup chopped peanuts
- 2 heads Boston lettuce, cored, washed and separated into large leaves
- Whole fresh chives

**Asian chili sauce is a spicy condiment made from sun-dried chiles. It is often called Sriracha and can be found in the ethnic section of some large supermarkets and in Asian or specialty markets.*

1. Heat oil in large skillet over medium heat. Brown chicken in skillet, stirring to break up meat. Drain off any fat. Add tofu, bell pepper, green onions, ginger and garlic; cook and stir until green onions are softened. Add beer, hoisin sauce and chili sauce; cook until heated through. Stir in peanuts.

2. Place spoonful of chicken mixture in center of each lettuce leaf. Roll up to enclose filling. Wrap chives around filled leaves and tie to secure.

Makes about 20 wraps

CRISPY TORTILLA CHICKEN

- 1½ cups crushed tortilla chips
- 1 package (about 1 ounce) taco seasoning mix
- 3 pounds chicken wings, tips removed and cut into halves
- Salsa

1. Preheat oven to 350°F. Spray baking sheet with nonstick cooking spray.

2. Combine tortilla chips and seasoning mix in large shallow bowl. Coat chicken with crumb mixture, turning to coat all sides. Shake off excess crumbs; place chicken on prepared baking sheet.

3. Bake 40 minutes or until chicken is cooked through. Serve with salsa.

Makes 6 to 8 servings

Variation: The recipe can also be prepared using 1 pound boneless skinless chicken breasts cut into 1-inch strips. Bake in preheated 350°F oven 20 minutes or until chicken is cooked through.

SAUTÉED CHICKEN TENDERS WITH CINNAMON APPLESAUCE

- 2 tablespoons butter, divided
- 3 pounds apples, peeled, cored and cut into ½-inch slices
- 1 teaspoon ground cinnamon
- 1 egg, lightly beaten
- ¾ cup all-purpose flour
- ¾ teaspoon salt
- ¼ teaspoon black pepper
- 12 chicken tenders (about 1¾ pounds)
- 2 tablespoons olive oil, divided

1. Melt 1 tablespoon butter in large saucepan over medium heat. Add apples and cinnamon; cook 40 minutes or until most of the apples have broken down, stirring occasionally. Add 1 cup water after 25 minutes if sauce is too thick and beginning to brown. If you prefer smooth applesauce, transfer to blender and process until smooth.

2. Meanwhile, pour egg into shallow dish. Mix flour, salt and pepper in another shallow dish.

3. Place chicken tenders in egg, turning to coat; shake off excess egg. Dip chicken tenders, 1 at a time, into flour mixture, turning to coat.

4. Heat 1½ teaspoons butter and 1 tablespoon olive oil in large nonstick skillet over medium-high heat. Add half of chicken, making sure not to crowd pan; cook 6 minutes or until golden brown and cooked through, turning once. Transfer to paper towels to drain. Repeat with remaining chicken, adding remaining butter and oil as needed. Serve hot with applesauce. *Makes 4 to 6 servings*

Cook's Tip: To make applesauce, you can use almost any type of apple. Depending on the variety, the results will vary in sweetness and chunkiness. Braeburn apples are a good option; they break down and are fairly sweet. You can add ¼ to ½ cup of light brown sugar at the end to adjust the sweetness to your taste.

SPICY ALMOND CHICKEN WINGS

3 pounds chicken wings, tips removed and cut into halves
3 tablespoons vegetable oil
2 tablespoons jerk seasoning
½ teaspoon salt
1 cup slivered almonds, finely chopped

1. Place chicken wings in large bowl. Combine oil, seasoning and salt in small bowl; stir until blended. Pour over chicken; toss to coat. Cover and refrigerate 20 to 30 minutes.

2. Preheat oven to 400°F. Line baking sheet with foil. Spray with nonstick cooking spray.

3. Place almonds in shallow bowl. Roll chicken in almonds until coated. Place on prepared baking sheet. Bake 30 to 35 minutes or until cooked through. *Makes 6 to 8 servings*

DIJON CHICKEN SKEWERS

1 cup barbecue sauce
¼ cup Dijon mustard
1 pound chicken tenders (about 12)
Salt and black pepper

1. Soak 12 (10- to 12-inch) wooden skewers 20 minutes in cold water to prevent them from scorching; drain. Preheat broiler.

2. Combine barbecue sauce and mustard in medium bowl. Weave chicken tenders onto skewers; season with salt and pepper. Brush skewers with sauce mixture. Discard any remaining sauce mixture.

3. Broil skewers 12 to 14 minutes or until cooked through, turning once. *Makes 12 skewers*

Prep Time: 20 minutes
Cook Time: 12 to 14 minutes

PESTO CHICKEN BRUSCHETTA

- 2 tablespoons olive oil, divided
- 1 teaspoon coarsely chopped garlic, divided
- 8 diagonal slices (¼ inch thick) sourdough bread
- ½ cup (2 ounces) grated BELGIOIOSO® Asiago Cheese, divided
- 2 tablespoons prepared pesto
- ¼ teaspoon pepper
- 4 boneless skinless chicken breast halves
- 12 slices (¼ inch thick) BELGIOIOSO® Fresh Mozzarella Cheese (8 ounces)
- 2 tomatoes, each cut into 4 slices

In 10-inch skillet, heat 1 tablespoon olive oil and ½ teaspoon garlic. Add 4 slices bread. Cook over medium-high heat, turning once, 5 to 7 minutes or until toasted. Remove from pan. Add remaining 1 tablespoon oil and ½ teaspoon garlic; repeat with remaining bread slices. Sprinkle ¼ cup BELGIOIOSO® Asiago Cheese on bread. In same skillet, combine pesto and pepper. Add chicken, coating with pesto. Cook over medium-high heat, turning once, 8 to 10 minutes or until chicken is brown. Place 3 slices BELGIOIOSO® Fresh Mozzarella Cheese on each bread slice; top with tomato slice. Slice chicken pieces in half horizontally; place on tomato. Sprinkle with remaining BELGIOIOSO® Asiago Cheese.

Makes 4 servings

STUFFED MUSHROOM CAPS

- 2 packages (8 ounces each) whole mushrooms
- 1 tablespoon butter
- ⅔ cup finely chopped cooked chicken
- ¼ cup grated Parmesan cheese
- 1 tablespoon chopped fresh basil
- 2 teaspoons fresh lemon juice
- ⅛ teaspoon onion powder
- ⅛ teaspoon salt
- Pinch garlic powder
- Pinch black pepper
- 1 package (3 ounces) cream cheese, softened
- Paprika (optional)

1. Preheat oven to 350°F. Remove stems from mushrooms and finely chop. Arrange mushroom caps on greased baking sheet.

2. Melt butter in medium skillet over medium-high heat; cook chopped mushrooms 5 minutes. Add chicken, Parmesan cheese, basil, lemon juice, onion powder, salt, garlic powder and pepper; cook and stir 5 minutes. Remove from heat; stir in cream cheese.

3. Spoon mixture into mushroom caps. Bake 10 to 15 minutes or until heated through. Sprinkle with paprika, if desired.

Makes about 26 stuffed mushrooms

MOROCCAN CHICKEN TURNOVERS

- ½ cup (1 stick) plus 2 tablespoons butter, divided
- ⅔ cup finely chopped onion
- ½ cup finely chopped carrots
- 1½ teaspoons grated fresh ginger
- ½ teaspoon salt
- ½ teaspoon dried oregano
- ½ teaspoon ground cumin
- ¼ teaspoon paprika
- ⅛ teaspoon ground red pepper
- ⅓ cup water
- ¼ cup tomato paste
- 2 cups finely chopped cooked chicken
- 16 sheets frozen phyllo dough, thawed

1. Melt 2 tablespoons butter in medium skillet over medium heat. Add onion and carrots; cook 6 to 8 minutes or until very soft, stirring frequently. Add ginger, salt, oregano, cumin, paprika and red pepper; cook and stir 1 minute. Stir in water and tomato paste until well blended. Add chicken; cook and stir 2 minutes. (Mixture will be very thick.) Spread filling in shallow pan; place in freezer 15 minutes to cool. (Filling may be prepared up to 24 hours in advance; cover and store in refrigerator.)

2. Preheat oven to 350°F. Melt remaining ½ cup butter. Stack 4 sheets phyllo on clean work surface or cutting board, brushing each with melted butter before adding next sheet. Cut phyllo stack in 4 strips lengthwise.

3. Place 1 heaping tablespoonful filling about 1 inch from bottom of each strip. Fold one corner of phyllo diagonally across to opposite edge to form triangle; continue to fold triangle up as you would fold a flag. Arrange triangles seam side down, at least 1 inch apart, on ungreased baking sheet; brush tops with melted butter. Repeat with remaining phyllo, filling and melted butter.

4. Bake 15 minutes or until golden brown.

Makes 16 turnovers

DIM SUM BAKED BUNS

9 frozen bread dough dinner rolls
6 to 8 dried shiitake mushrooms
3 green onions, minced
2 tablespoons plum sauce
1 tablespoon hoisin sauce
Nonstick cooking spray
8 ounces ground chicken
4 cloves garlic, minced
1 tablespoon minced fresh ginger
1 egg, lightly beaten
¾ teaspoon sesame seeds

1. Thaw frozen rolls according to package directions.

2. Place mushrooms in small bowl. Cover with warm water; let stand 30 minutes. Rinse well and drain, squeezing out excess water. Cut off and discard stems. Finely chop caps. Combine mushrooms, green onions, plum sauce and hoisin sauce in medium bowl.

3. Spray medium nonstick skillet with cooking spray; heat over high heat. Add chicken; brown 1 to 2 minutes, stirring to break up meat. Add garlic and ginger; cook and stir 2 minutes or until chicken is cooked through. Add mushroom mixture; mix well.

4. Spray 2 baking sheets with cooking spray. Lightly flour hands and work surface. Cut each roll in half; roll each piece into ball. Shape each piece between hands to form disk. Press edge of disk between thumb and forefinger, working in circular motion to form circle 3 to 3½ inches in diameter (center of disk should be thicker than edges).

5. Place dough on work surface. Place 1 heaping tablespoonful filling in center. Lift edges of dough up and around filling; pinch edges of dough together to seal. Place seam side down on baking sheet. Repeat with remaining dough and filling.

6. Cover buns with towel; let rise in warm place 45 minutes or until buns have doubled in size. Meanwhile, preheat oven to 375°F. Brush buns with egg; sprinkle with sesame seeds. Bake 16 to 18 minutes or until golden brown.

Makes 18 buns

SPANISH TORTILLA

- 1 teaspoon olive oil
- 1 cup thinly sliced peeled potato
- 1 small zucchini, thinly sliced
- ¼ cup chopped onion
- 1 clove garlic, minced
- 1 cup shredded cooked chicken
- 8 eggs
- ½ teaspoon salt
- ½ teaspoon black pepper
- ¼ teaspoon red pepper flakes
- Salsa (optional)

1. Heat oil in 10-inch nonstick skillet over medium-high heat. Add potatoes, zucchini, onion and garlic; cook 5 minutes or until potato is tender, stirring frequently. Stir in chicken; cook 1 minute.

2. Meanwhile, whisk eggs, salt, black pepper and pepper flakes in large bowl. Pour egg mixture into skillet. Reduce heat to low; cover and cook 12 to 15 minutes or until center is set.

3. Loosen edges of tortilla and slide onto large serving platter. Let stand 5 minutes before cutting into wedges or 1-inch cubes. Serve warm or at room temperature. Serve with salsa, if desired.

Makes 10 to 12 servings

TIP In Spanish, tortilla means "flat cake." Similar to an Italian frittata, these thick omelets are a popular snack throughout Spain. They can be filled with a variety of tasty ingredients, however, the most traditional filling is potatoes fried in olive oil.

CHICKEN WINGS WITH CHIVE–CAPER MAYONNAISE

- ⅓ cup mayonnaise
- 1 tablespoon minced fresh chives
- 2 teaspoons capers
- ¼ teaspoon black pepper, divided
- ¼ cup all-purpose flour
- ½ teaspoon paprika, divided
- ¼ teaspoon salt
- 2 eggs
- ½ cup plain dry bread crumbs
- 1½ pounds chicken wings, tips removed and cut into halves
- 2 tablespoons butter
- 2 tablespoons vegetable oil

1. For Chive-Caper Mayonnaise, stir together mayonnaise, chives, capers and ⅛ teaspoon pepper in small bowl.

2. Combine flour, ¼ teaspoon paprika, salt and remaining ⅛ teaspoon pepper in large resealable food storage bag. Beat eggs in shallow bowl. Combine bread crumbs and remaining ¼ teaspoon paprika on large plate.

3. Add chicken to flour mixture; shake well to coat. Dip chicken in eggs, then roll in bread crumbs.

4. Heat butter and oil in large heavy skillet over medium-high heat until butter melts and mixture sizzles. Cook chicken 6 to 7 minutes or until browned on all sides, turning occasionally. Reduce heat to low; cook 5 minutes or until chicken is cooked through, turning occasionally. Serve with Chive-Caper Mayonnaise.

Makes 3 to 4 servings

BAKED EGG ROLLS

- Sesame Dipping Sauce (recipe follows)
- 1 ounce dried shiitake mushrooms
- 1 can (8 ounces) sliced water chestnuts, drained and minced
- 1 large carrot, shredded
- 3 green onions, minced
- 3 tablespoons chopped fresh cilantro
- Nonstick cooking spray
- 12 ounces ground chicken
- 2 tablespoons minced fresh ginger
- 6 cloves garlic, minced
- 2 tablespoons soy sauce
- 2 teaspoons water
- 1 teaspoon cornstarch
- 12 egg roll wrappers
- 1 tablespoon vegetable oil
- 1 teaspoon sesame seeds

1. Prepare Sesame Dipping Sauce; set aside.

2. Place mushrooms in small bowl. Cover with warm water; let stand 30 minutes or until tender. Rinse well; drain, squeezing out excess water. Cut off and discard stems. Finely chop caps; combine with water chestnuts, carrot, green onions and cilantro in large bowl.

3. Spray medium nonstick skillet with cooking spray; heat over high heat. Add chicken; cook and stir 2 minutes or until browned. Add ginger and garlic; cook and stir 2 minutes or until chicken is cooked through. Add to mushroom mixture. Sprinkle with soy sauce; mix thoroughly.

4. Preheat oven to 425°F. Spray baking sheet with cooking spray; set aside. Blend water and cornstarch in small bowl until smooth. Lay 1 wrapper on work surface. Spoon about ⅓ cup filling across center of wrapper to within about ½ inch of sides. Fold bottom of wrapper over filling. Fold in sides. Brush ½-inch strip across top edge with cornstarch mixture; roll up and seal. Place seam side down on baking sheet. Repeat with remaining wrappers.

5. Brush egg rolls with oil. Sprinkle with sesame seeds. Bake 18 minutes or until golden and crisp. Serve with Sesame Dipping Sauce. *Makes 6 servings*

Sesame Dipping Sauce: Combine ¼ cup rice vinegar, 2 teaspoons soy sauce, 1 teaspoon minced fresh ginger and 1 teaspoon dark sesame oil in small bowl. Makes 5 tablespoons.

BACON–WRAPPED BBQ CHICKEN

- **8 chicken tenders, patted dry (about 1 pound)**
- **½ teaspoon paprika or cumin**
- **8 slices bacon**
- **½ cup barbecue sauce, divided**

1. Preheat broiler. Line broiler pan with foil.

2. Sprinkle chicken tenders with paprika. Wrap each chicken tender with slice of bacon in spiral pattern; place on broiler pan.

3. Broil chicken 4 minutes. Turn and broil 2 minutes. Brush with ¼ cup barbecue sauce; broil 2 minutes. Turn and brush with remaining ¼ cup barbecue sauce. Broil 2 minutes or until chicken is no longer pink in center.

Makes 4 servings

SPICY CHICKEN STROMBOLI

- **1 cup frozen broccoli florets, thawed**
- **1 can (10 ounces) chunk white chicken packed in water, drained**
- **1½ cups (6 ounces) shredded Monterey Jack cheese with jalapeño peppers**
- **¼ cup chunky salsa**
- **2 green onions, chopped**
- **1 package (10 ounces) refrigerated pizza dough**

1. Preheat oven to 400°F. Coarsely chop broccoli. Combine broccoli, chicken, cheese, salsa and green onions in small bowl.

2. Unroll pizza dough. Pat into 15×10-inch rectangle. Sprinkle broccoli mixture evenly over top. Starting with long side, tightly roll up jelly-roll style. Pinch seam to seal. Place on baking sheet, seam side down.

3. Bake 15 to 20 minutes or until golden brown. Transfer to wire rack to cool slightly. Slice and serve warm.

Makes 6 servings

Serving Suggestion: Serve with additional salsa on the side for dipping.

Prep and Cook Time: 30 minutes

TORTILLA "PIZZAS"

- 1 can (about 14 ounces) Mexican-style stewed tomatoes, drained
- 1 can (10 ounces) chunk white chicken packed in water, drained
- 1 green onion, minced
- 2 teaspoons ground cumin, divided
- ½ teaspoon garlic powder
- 1 cup refried beans
- 4 tablespoons chopped fresh cilantro, divided
- 2 flour tortillas
- 1 cup (4 ounces) shredded Monterey Jack cheese with jalapeño peppers

1. Preheat broiler. Combine tomatoes, chicken, green onion, 1 teaspoon cumin and garlic powder in medium bowl. Stir together refried beans, 2 tablespoons cilantro and remaining 1 teaspoon cumin in small bowl.

2. Place tortillas on baking sheet. Broil 30 seconds per side or until crisp but not browned. Remove from oven. *Reduce oven temperature to 400°F.* Spread bean mixture evenly over each tortilla. Top with chicken mixture and cheese. Bake 5 minutes.

3. *Turn oven to broil.* Broil tortillas 2 to 3 minutes or until cheese melts. Do not let tortilla edges burn. Top with remaining cilantro. Serve immediately.

Makes 8 servings

CRISPY RANCH CHICKEN BITES

- Olive oil cooking spray
- 1 pound boneless skinless chicken breasts
- ¾ cup ranch dressing
- 2 cups panko bread crumbs

1. Preheat oven to 375°F. Line baking sheets with foil; spray foil with cooking spray.

2. Cut chicken into 1-inch cubes. Place ranch dressing in small bowl. Spread panko in shallow dish. Dip chicken in ranch dressing; shake off excess. Transfer chicken to panko; toss to coat, pressing panko into chicken. Place on prepared baking sheets.

3. Spray breaded chicken with cooking spray. Bake 15 to 17 minutes or until golden brown, turning once.

Makes 6 to 8 servings

CHICKEN SATAY SKEWERS

- 6 garlic cloves, chopped
- 4 teaspoons dried coriander
- 4 teaspoons light brown sugar
- 2 teaspoons salt
- 1½ teaspoons HERSHEY'S Cocoa
- 1 teaspoon ground black pepper
- ½ cup soy sauce
- 6 tablespoons vegetable oil
- 2 tablespoons lime juice
- 4 teaspoons fresh chopped ginger
- 2½ pounds boneless, skinless chicken breasts
- Peanut Dipping Sauce (recipe follows)
- ¼ cup fresh cilantro, chopped (optional)

1. Combine garlic, coriander, brown sugar, salt, cocoa and pepper in large bowl. Stir in soy sauce, oil, lime juice and ginger.

2. Cut chicken into 1½- to 2-inch cubes. Add to soy sauce mixture, stirring to coat chicken pieces. Cover; marinate in refrigerator for at least 2 hours.

3. Meanwhile, prepare Peanut Dipping Sauce. Thread chicken pieces onto skewers. Grill or broil, basting with marinade. Discard leftover marinade. Garnish with chopped cilantro, if desired. Serve with prepared peanut sauce. Refrigerate leftovers.

Makes 15 to 20 appetizers

PEANUT DIPPING SAUCE

- ½ cup peanut oil
- 1 cup REESE'S® Creamy Peanut Butter
- ¼ cup lime juice
- ¼ cup soy sauce
- 3 tablespoons honey
- 2 garlic cloves, minced
- 1 teaspoon cayenne pepper
- ½ teaspoon hot pepper sauce

Gradually whisk peanut oil into peanut butter in medium bowl. Blend in lime juice, soy sauce, honey, garlic, cayenne pepper and hot pepper sauce. Adjust flavors to taste for a sweet/hot flavor.

Makes 2¼ cups

CHICKEN GYOZA

4 ounces ground chicken
¼ cup finely chopped napa cabbage
1 green onion, minced
1½ teaspoons soy sauce
½ teaspoon minced fresh ginger
½ teaspoon cornstarch
22 gyoza or wonton wrappers (about half of 10-ounce package)
2 tablespoons vegetable oil
Dipping Sauce (recipe follows)

1. Combine chicken, cabbage, green onion, soy sauce and ginger in medium bowl. Add cornstarch; stir.

2. Place 1 rounded teaspoonful chicken filling in center of gyoza wrapper. Dampen edges of wrapper with wet finger. Pull sides of wrapper together; press to seal semicircle. Pleat edges of gyoza by making small folds. Place on lightly oiled surface while filling remaining gyoza.

3. Heat oil in large skillet over medium heat. Add 8 to 10 gyoza to skillet; do not crowd pan. Cook 3 minutes per side until golden brown and filling is cooked through. Keep warm while frying remaining gyoza. Serve with Dipping Sauce.

Makes 22 gyoza

Dipping Sauce: Combine ¼ cup soy sauce, 2 teaspoons mirin (Japanese sweet rice wine) and ¼ to ½ teaspoon chili oil in small bowl. Stir well. Makes about ¼ cup.

SZECHUAN CHICKEN TENDERS

2 tablespoons soy sauce
1 tablespoon Asian chili sauce*
1 tablespoon dry sherry
2 cloves garlic, minced
¼ teaspoon red pepper flakes
16 chicken tenders (about 1 pound)
1 tablespoon peanut oil

**Asian chili sauce is a spicy condiment made from sun-dried chiles. It is often called Sriracha and can be found in the ethnic section of some large supermarkets and in Asian or specialty markets.*

Combine soy sauce, chili sauce, sherry, garlic and pepper flakes in shallow dish. Add chicken; coat well. Heat oil in large nonstick skillet over medium heat. Add chicken; cook 6 minutes or until browned and cooked through, turning occasionally.

Makes 4 servings

CHEESY CHICKEN NACHOS

- 2 tablespoons olive oil
- 1 onion, diced
- 1 teaspoon POLANER® Chopped Garlic
- 1 pound ground chicken
- 1 jar (16 ounces) ORTEGA® Salsa, any variety, divided
- 2 teaspoons dried parsley
- 1 teaspoon ORTEGA® Chili Seasoning Mix
- 1 teaspoon REGINA® Red Wine Vinegar
- ½ cup water
- 12 ORTEGA® Yellow Corn Taco Shells, broken
- 1 pound shredded taco cheese blend (4 cups)
- 1 can (15 ounces) JOAN OF ARC® Black Beans
- 1 jar (12 ounces) ORTEGA® Sliced Jalapeños

Heat oil in skillet over medium-high heat until hot. Add onion and garlic. Cook and stir until onions are translucent, about 3 minutes. Stir in chicken, ¾ cup salsa, parsley, seasoning mix, vinegar and ½ cup water; cook until meat is cooked through and sauce begins to thicken, about 5 minutes.

Preheat broiler; place rack about 7 inches from top of oven.

Assemble nachos by arranging broken taco shells on baking sheet. Sprinkle on 2 cups cheese; top with chicken mixture, black beans and jalapeños. Add remaining salsa and cheese. (If desired, prepare individual portions by dividing recipe among 6 heat-resistant plates.)

Place under broiler 4 minutes or until cheese begins to melt. *Makes 6 servings*

Note: Be sure to have some of your favorite guacamole, sour cream and black olives on hand to place on top of the nachos.

Prep Time: 10 minutes
Start-to-Finish Time: 20 minutes

CHICKEN PESTO PIZZA

- Cornmeal
- 1 loaf (1 pound) frozen bread dough, thawed
- Nonstick cooking spray
- 8 ounces chicken tenders, cut into ½-inch pieces
- ½ red onion, cut into quarters and thinly sliced
- ¼ cup prepared pesto
- 2 large plum tomatoes, seeded and diced
- 1 cup (4 ounces) shredded pizza cheese blend or mozzarella cheese

1. Preheat oven to 375°F. Sprinkle baking sheet with cornmeal. Roll out dough on floured surface to 14×8-inch rectangle. Transfer to prepared baking sheet. Cover loosely with plastic wrap; let rise 20 to 30 minutes.

2. Meanwhile, spray large skillet with cooking spray; heat over medium heat. Add chicken; cook and stir 2 minutes. Add onion and pesto; cook and stir 3 to 4 minutes or until chicken is cooked through. Stir in tomatoes. Remove from heat; let cool slightly.

3. Spread chicken mixture evenly over dough to within 1 inch of edges. Sprinkle with cheese. Bake on bottom rack 20 minutes or until crust is golden brown. Cut into 2-inch squares. *Makes 28 pieces*

CARIBBEAN CHICKEN QUESADILLAS

- 2 cups shredded cooked chicken
- ¼ cup *Frank's® RedHot® Chile 'n Lime™* Hot Sauce
- ¼ teaspoon ground cinnamon
- 8 (8-inch) flour tortillas
- 2 cups shredded Monterey Jack cheese
- ½ cup thinly sliced green onions

1. Combine chicken, *Chile 'n Lime™* Hot Sauce and cinnamon in medium bowl.

2. Top 4 tortillas with cheese, green onions and chicken mixture, dividing evenly. Cover each with another tortilla, pressing down firmly.

3. Heat an electric grill pan until hot; coat with vegetable cooking spray. Cook quesadillas over medium heat about 2 to 3 minutes until golden, turning once. Cut into wedges to serve. *Makes 4 servings*

• CHICKEN PESTO PIZZA •

APRICOT–CHICKEN POT STICKERS

- 2 cups plus 1 tablespoon water, divided
- 2 boneless skinless chicken breasts (about 8 ounces)
- 2 cups finely chopped cabbage
- ½ cup apricot fruit spread
- 2 green onions, finely chopped
- 2 teaspoons soy sauce
- ½ teaspoon grated fresh ginger
- ⅛ teaspoon black pepper
- 30 (3-inch) wonton wrappers
- Sweet and sour sauce (optional)

1. Bring 2 cups water to a boil in medium saucepan. Add chicken. Reduce heat to low; simmer, covered, 10 minutes or until chicken is no longer pink in center. Set aside chicken; drain saucepan.

2. Add cabbage and remaining 1 tablespoon water to same saucepan. Cook over high heat 1 to 2 minutes or until water evaporates, stirring occasionally. Remove from heat; cool slightly.

3. Finely chop chicken; return to saucepan. Add fruit spread, green onions, soy sauce, ginger and pepper; mix well.

4. To assemble pot stickers, remove 3 wonton wrappers at a time from package. Spoon slightly rounded tablespoonful chicken mixture onto center of each wrapper; brush edges of wrapper with water. Bring 4 corners together; press to seal. Repeat with remaining wrappers and filling.

5. Spray steamer basket with nonstick cooking spray. Assemble steamer, adding water up to ½ inch below steamer basket. Fill basket with pot stickers, leaving enough space between to prevent sticking. Cover; steam 5 minutes. Transfer pot stickers to serving plate. Serve with sweet and sour sauce, if desired.

Makes 10 servings

BOMBAY CHICKEN WINGS

- 2 (1 ¼ pound) packages chicken wing drummettes (24 pieces)
- 1 teaspoon curry powder
- ½ teaspoon ground turmeric
- 2 tablespoons soy sauce
- 2 tablespoons vegetable oil
- 2 tablespoons green onion, minced
- 2 cloves garlic, minced
- ⅛ teaspoon black pepper
- Sprigs of cilantro for garnish
- Yogurt Chutney Dipping Sauce (recipe follows)

In large bowl, mix all ingredients except chicken wings and cilantro to make marinade. Add chicken wings, making sure all pieces are coated well with mixture; cover and refrigerate for at least 1 hour.

Prepare Yogurt Chutney Dipping Sauce. Preheat oven to 360°F. Drain chicken wings; place in single layer on jelly-roll pan. Bake 25 minutes or until golden brown. Arrange on platter surrounding a bowl of Yogurt Chutney Dipping Sauce. Garnish with cilantro sprigs and serve. *Makes 24 appetizers*

Favorite recipe from National Chicken Council

YOGURT CHUTNEY DIPPING SAUCE

- ½ cup plain yogurt
- 3 tablespoons mango, finely chopped
- 1 tablespoon cilantro, minced
- 1 tablespoon green onion, minced
- ¼ teaspoon hot sauce
- ⅛ teaspoon salt

In medium bowl, combine all ingredients. Cover and refrigerate until needed. *Makes about ¾ cup*

Favorite recipe from National Chicken Council

CHICKEN MEATBALLS WITH CHIPOTLE–HONEY SAUCE

- 2 pounds ground chicken
- 2 eggs, lightly beaten
- ⅓ cup plain dry bread crumbs
- ⅓ cup chopped fresh cilantro
- 2 tablespoons fresh lime juice
- 4 cloves garlic, minced
- 1 can (4 ounces) chipotle peppers in adobo sauce, divided
- 1 teaspoon salt
- Chipotle-Honey Sauce (recipe follows)
- 2 tablespoons vegetable oil

1. Line 2 baking sheets with parchment paper. Combine chicken, eggs, bread crumbs, cilantro, lime juice, garlic, 1 tablespoon adobo sauce and salt in medium bowl; mix well. Form mixture into 48 meatballs. Place meatballs on prepared baking sheets. Cover with plastic wrap; chill 1 hour.

2. Prepare Chipotle-Honey Sauce. Preheat oven to 400°F. Lightly coat meatballs with oil using pastry brush. Bake 12 minutes. Transfer meatballs to baking dish. Add sauce; stir until coated. Bake 10 minutes or until meatballs are heated through and glazed with sauce. *Makes 48 meatballs*

CHIPOTLE–HONEY SAUCE

- ¾ cup honey
- 2 to 3 whole chipotle peppers in adobo sauce
- ⅓ cup chicken broth
- ⅓ cup tomato paste
- 1 tablespoon fresh lime juice
- 2 teaspoons Dijon mustard
- ½ teaspoon salt

Combine all ingredients in food processor or blender; process until smooth. *Makes 1½ cups*

CHICKEN CORNDOG BITES

- 1 can (11½ ounces) refrigerated corn breadstick dough (8 breadsticks)
- 1 package (10 ounces) Italian-seasoned cooked chicken breast strips
- Mustard
- Ketchup

1. Preheat oven to 375°F. Line baking sheet with parchment paper or foil.

2. Unroll dough and separate into individual breadsticks. Roll out each breadstick into 7×1½-inch rectangle. Cut each rectangle in half crosswise to form 16 pieces total. Cut chicken strips in half crosswise. Place one piece chicken on each piece dough; wrap dough around chicken and seal, pressing edges together tightly. Place seam side down on prepared baking sheet.

3. Bake 15 to 17 minutes or until golden brown. Serve with mustard and ketchup. *Makes 16 pieces*

HONDURAN CHICKEN SKEWERS

- ¼ cup BERTOLLI® Olive Oil
- 1 small onion, chopped
- ¼ cup tightly packed cilantro leaves
- 4 teaspoons KNORR® Reduced Sodium Chicken flavor Bouillon
- 1 tablespoon chopped canned chipotle chilies in adobo sauce
- 1 tablespoon sugar
- 2 cloves garlic
- ½ cup HELLMANN'S® or BEST FOODS® Real Mayonnaise
- 1 pound boneless, skinless chicken breast halves, cut into strips

Process first 7 ingredients in a blender or food processor until smooth. Remove 1 tablespoon of mixture and combine with Mayonnaise. Refrigerate until ready to use.

Thread chicken onto 8 skewers and arrange in a large nonaluminum baking dish; rub with remaining olive oil mixture. Cover and marinate in refrigerator about 30 minutes.

Grill or broil chicken about 6 minutes or until chicken is thoroughly cooked, turning once. Serve with mayonnaise dipping sauce. *Makes 4 servings*

CHICKEN BITES WITH ORANGE–WALNUT SAUCE

- ½ cup orange marmalade
- 3 tablespoons orange juice
- 2 tablespoons chopped walnuts
- 2 pitted prunes, chopped
- 1 tablespoon raisins
- ¼ teaspoon black pepper, divided
- 2 boneless skinless chicken breasts, cut into 1-inch cubes
- Grated peel and juice of 1 orange
- 3 tablespoons olive oil, divided
- 2 tablespoons Spanish sherry
- ½ teaspoon salt

1. For Orange-Walnut Sauce, combine marmalade, 3 tablespoons orange juice, walnuts, prunes, raisins and ⅛ teaspoon pepper in small microwavable bowl. Microwave on HIGH 1 minute; stir until blended.

2. Place chicken in medium bowl; sprinkle with orange peel and juice. Add 1 tablespoon oil, sherry, salt and remaining ⅛ teaspoon pepper; toss to coat.

3. Heat remaining 2 tablespoons oil in medium nonstick skillet over medium heat. Using slotted spoon, transfer chicken to skillet. Cook 5 to 6 minutes or until browned on all sides and chicken is cooked through. Add any remaining marinade. Bring to a boil; boil 1 minute. Remove chicken and pan juices to serving plate. Serve chicken drizzled with Orange-Walnut Sauce.

Makes 6 servings

Note: The sauce can be prepared, covered and refrigerated for up to two days in advance. Allow to come to room temperature before serving.

HONEY–MUSTARD CHICKEN WINGS

- 3 pounds chicken wings, tips removed and cut into halves
- 1 teaspoon salt
- 1 teaspoon black pepper
- ½ cup honey
- ½ cup barbecue sauce
- 2 tablespoons spicy brown mustard
- 1 clove garlic, minced
- 3 to 4 thin lemon slices

continued on page 46

Honey-Mustard Chicken Wings, continued

Slow Cooker Directions

1. Preheat broiler. Sprinkle chicken wings with salt and pepper; place on broiler rack. Broil 4 to 5 inches from heat 10 minutes, turning once. Place in 6-quart slow cooker.

2. Combine honey, barbecue sauce, mustard and garlic in small bowl; mix well. Pour over chicken wings. Top with lemon slices. Cover; cook on LOW 4 to 5 hours.

3. Remove and discard lemon slices. Serve wings with sauce.

Makes 6 to 8 servings

Prep Time: 20 minutes
Cook Time: 4 to 5 hours

CHICKEN FLAUTAS

2 tablespoons olive oil
1 onion, diced
½ of (1½- to 2-pound) cooked rotisserie chicken, bones removed and meat shredded
½ cup ORTEGA® Salsa, any variety
6 ORTEGA® Flour Tortillas
½ cup canola oil

Heat olive oil in skillet over medium-high heat until hot. Add onion; cook and stir until tender. Add shredded chicken and salsa; toss together. Remove from heat.

Place several tablespoons of chicken mixture in middle of tortilla and firmly roll like a cigar. Keep tortilla roll closed with 2 toothpicks. Repeat with remaining tortillas.

Heat canola oil in skillet over medium-high heat until hot. Fry tortilla rolls in oil for several minutes in small batches until tortillas begin to brown. Turn over and continue frying until all sides are browned, about 4 minutes. Remove tortilla rolls from oil and drain on paper towels.

Remove toothpicks and cut each flauta on the bias to serve.

Makes 6 servings

Prep Time: 5 minutes
Start-to-Finish Time: 20 minutes

SAVORY SALADS

COBB SALAD

1 package (10 ounces) torn mixed salad greens *or* 8 cups torn romaine lettuce
6 ounces chopped cooked chicken
1 tomato, seeded and chopped
2 hard-cooked eggs, cut into bite-size pieces
4 slices bacon, crisp-cooked and crumbled
1 ripe avocado, peeled and diced
1 large carrot, cut into matchstick-size strips
2 ounces blue cheese, crumbled
Vinaigrette dressing (optional)

1. Place lettuce in serving bowl. Arrange chicken, tomato, eggs, bacon, avocado, carrot and cheese on top of lettuce.

2. Serve with dressing, if desired.

Makes 4 servings

Prep Time: 15 minutes

SINGAPORE CHICKEN SALAD

Singapore Dressing (recipe follows)
1 tablespoon ground cumin
½ teaspoon salt
½ teaspoon ground nutmeg
½ teaspoon ground red pepper
½ teaspoon turmeric
¼ teaspoon ground cinnamon
1½ pounds boneless skinless chicken breasts
4 cups water
1 small head cauliflower (about 1¼ pounds), broken into florets
4 large carrots, cut into matchstick-size strips
1 cup vegetable oil
8 wonton wrappers, cut into ¼-inch-wide strips
4 cups shredded romaine lettuce
8 ounces fresh bean sprouts, rinsed and drained

1. Prepare Singapore Dressing. Place cumin, salt, nutmeg, red pepper, turmeric and cinnamon in wok or large deep skillet; mix well. Cook and stir over medium heat 30 seconds or until fragrant; transfer to large bowl. Add chicken and stir until well coated; set aside.

2. Place water in wok; bring to a boil over high heat. Add cauliflower; cook 3 minutes or just until crisp-tender. Remove with slotted spoon to bowl of cold water. Add carrot strips to boiling water; cook 4 minutes or until crisp-tender. Drain carrots; rinse with cold water. Drain cauliflower.

3. Heat wok over medium-high heat until dry. Add oil and heat until 350°F on deep-fry thermometer. Add wonton strips, a handful at a time, and fry 10 to 15 seconds or until golden brown, stirring with slotted spoon. Remove strips to tray or plate lined with paper towels; drain.

4. Drain all but 1 tablespoon oil from wok; heat over medium-high heat 30 seconds. Add chicken and spice mixture; cook 4 minutes or until browned, turning once. Cover and reduce heat to low. Cook 6 minutes or until no longer pink in center. Transfer chicken to cutting board. Slice across grain when cool.

5. Place lettuce on large serving platter. Top with chicken, cauliflower, carrots and sprouts. Pour dressing over chicken. Serve with fried wonton strips. *Makes 6 servings*

Singapore Dressing: Whisk together ⅓ cup rice vinegar, 3 tablespoons vegetable oil, 2 tablespoons hoisin sauce, 1 tablespoon dark sesame oil and 1 teaspoon sugar in small bowl. Cover and refrigerate until serving. Makes about ¾ cup.

MILD CURRY CHICKEN SALAD WITH FRUIT

2 cups (1 pint) prepared creamy chicken salad
2 teaspoons sugar
1½ to 2 teaspoons curry powder
⅛ teaspoon ground red pepper (optional)
Fresh pineapple wedges

1. Combine chicken salad, sugar, curry powder and red pepper, if desired, in medium bowl. Stir gently until well blended.

2. Spoon salad evenly onto plates. Serve with pineapple. *Makes 2 servings*

Variations: Try adding 2 tablespoons of currants, chopped apples, sliced red grapes, sliced green onions or toasted slivered almonds to give the salad extra color and crunch. Serve on a bed of spring greens or baby spinach leaves for a complete meal.

CHICKEN AND COUSCOUS VEGETABLE SALAD

1½ cups low-sodium chicken broth
1 cup uncooked couscous
1½ cups chopped cooked chicken or turkey
½ pound DOLE® Asparagus, cut into 1-inch pieces, cooked and drained
1½ cups chopped green or yellow bell pepper
1 medium tomato, chopped
½ cup sliced DOLE® Celery
½ cup fat-free or light Italian salad dressing
2 tablespoons sliced almonds, toasted

• Pour broth in saucepan; bring to boil. Stir in couscous. Remove from heat; cover, let stand 5 minutes. Stir with fork.

• Stir together couscous, chicken, asparagus, bell pepper, tomato and celery in bowl.

• Add dressing; stir to evenly coat salad. Serve at room temperature or chilled. Sprinkle with almonds just before serving. *Makes 6 servings*

Prep Time: 25 minutes
Cook Time: 10 minutes

• MILD CURRY CHICKEN SALAD WITH FRUIT •

CHICKEN, TORTELLINI & ROASTED VEGETABLE SALAD

- Sun-Dried Tomato & Basil Vinaigrette (recipe follows)
- 3 cups whole medium mushrooms
- 2 cups cubed zucchini
- 2 cups cubed eggplant
- 1 red onion, cut into wedges
- Olive oil cooking spray
- 1½ (9-ounce) packages cheese tortellini
- 6 cups leaf lettuce and arugula
- 1 pound deli chicken breast, cut into 1½-inch pieces

1. Preheat oven to 425°F. Prepare Sun-Dried Tomato & Basil Vinaigrette.

2. Place mushrooms, zucchini, eggplant and onion in 15×10-inch jelly-roll pan. Spray vegetables generously with cooking spray; toss to coat. Bake 20 to 25 minutes or until vegetables are browned. Lightly spray with cooking spray; cool to room temperature.

3. Meanwhile, cook tortellini according to package directions; drain. Cool to room temperature.

4. Combine vegetables, tortellini, lettuce mixture and chicken in large bowl. Drizzle with Sun-Dried Tomato & Basil Vinaigrette; toss to coat.

Makes 8 servings

SUN-DRIED TOMATO & BASIL VINAIGRETTE

- 4 sun-dried tomato halves, not packed in oil
- Boiling water
- ½ cup chicken broth
- 2 tablespoons finely chopped fresh basil *or* 2 teaspoons dried basil
- 2 tablespoons water
- 2 tablespoons fresh lemon juice
- 2 tablespoons olive oil
- 1 clove garlic, minced
- ¼ teaspoon salt
- ¼ teaspoon black pepper

1. Place tomatoes in small bowl; cover with boiling water. Let stand 5 to 10 minutes or until soft. Drain well; chop.

2. Combine tomatoes and remaining ingredients in small jar with tight-fitting lid; shake well. Chill until ready to use; shake before using.

Makes about 1 cup

PAELLA SALAD

Garlic Dressing (recipe follows)
2½ cups water
1 cup uncooked rice
1 teaspoon salt
¼ to ½ teaspoon powdered saffron or turmeric
2 cups cubed cooked chicken
4 ounces medium cooked shrimp, peeled and deveined
1 cup diced drained canned artichoke hearts
½ cup cooked peas
2 tablespoons chopped salami
2 tablespoons thinly sliced green onion
2 tablespoons chopped drained pimiento
1 tablespoon minced fresh parsley
Lettuce leaves
1 large tomato, seeded and cubed (optional)

1. Prepare Garlic Dressing; set aside.

2. Bring water to a boil in medium saucepan over high heat. Stir rice, salt and saffron into water. Reduce heat; cover and simmer 20 minutes. Remove from heat; let stand 5 minutes or until water is absorbed. Refrigerate 15 minutes or until cool.

3. Place rice, chicken, shrimp, artichoke hearts, peas, salami, green onion, pimiento and parsley in large bowl; toss well. Pour Garlic Dressing over salad; toss lightly to coat. Cover; refrigerate 1 hour.

4. Arrange lettuce on large serving platter or individual serving plates; top with salad mixture. Garnish with tomato.

Makes 4 to 6 servings

GARLIC DRESSING

¾ cup olive or vegetable oil
¼ cup white wine vinegar
1 clove garlic, pressed
1 teaspoon salt
½ teaspoon black pepper

Whisk together all ingredients in small bowl. Cover and refrigerate up to 2 weeks.

Makes 1 cup

ISLAND CHICKEN SALAD WITH BRILLIANT SPICE DRESSING

- 1 cup Brilliant Spice Dressing (recipe follows)
- ¾ pound cooked chicken, cut into small pieces
- 3 cups diced unpared red or green apples
- 2 cups diced pared pears
- 2 cups seedless red grapes
- 1 cup chopped green bell pepper
- 1 cup finely chopped green onion tops
- ½ cup minced celery
- 2 teaspoons Chef Paul Prudhomme's Poultry Magic®

Make Brilliant Spice Dressing. Combine 1 cup dressing with remaining ingredients in large salad bowl and toss to mix well. Cover and refrigerate until ready to serve. Allow 2 cups salad per serving.

Makes 4 servings

BRILLIANT SPICE DRESSING

- 2 tablespoons Chef Paul Prudhomme's Poultry Magic®
- 1 teaspoon ground turmeric
- 1 teaspoon dry mustard
- 1 teaspoon ground ginger
- 1 very ripe medium banana
- ¼ cup cider vinegar
- ¼ cup orange marmalade
- ¼ cup mayonnaise

Make a seasoning mix by thoroughly combining Poultry Magic®, turmeric, mustard and ginger in a small bowl; reserve. In blender or food processor fitted with metal blade, process banana until smooth. Add vinegar, marmalade, mayonnaise and seasoning mix; process until blended. With the motor running, slowly pour in oil until oil is incorporated and dressing is thick and creamy. Cover and refrigerate until ready to use. (Use 1 cup for Island Chicken Salad. Reserve remaining dressing for another use.)

Makes about 1⅔ cups

GINGER–TERIYAKI SALAD WITH FRIED CHICKEN TENDERS

- ¼ cup teriyaki sauce
- 3 tablespoons sugar
- 3 tablespoons cider vinegar
- 2 tablespoons dark sesame oil
- 1½ teaspoons minced fresh ginger
- ⅛ teaspoon red pepper flakes
- 1 bag (5 ounces) spring greens
- 1 cup broccoli florets
- 1 cup shredded carrots
- ½ cup chopped green onions
- 12 ounces fried chicken tenders, cut into ½-inch strips
- ¼ cup peanuts, toasted*

** To toast peanuts, spread in single layer in small skillet. Heat over medium-high heat 3 to 5 minutes or until fragrant, stirring frequently.*

1. For dressing, whisk together teriyaki sauce, sugar, vinegar, oil, ginger, and pepper flakes in small bowl.

2. Combine spring greens, broccoli, carrots and green onions in large bowl. Add dressing; toss to coat.

3. Spoon salad onto plates; top with chicken and peanuts.

Makes 2 servings

CHICKEN & RASPBERRY SALAD

- 2 containers (6 ounces each) red raspberries, divided
- ¼ cup honey
- 1 tablespoon balsamic vinegar
- Salt and black pepper
- 8 cups spring greens
- 4 boneless skinless chicken breasts, cooked and thinly sliced
- ¼ cup chopped walnuts

1. Combine 1 container raspberries, honey and vinegar in food processor or blender. Process using on/off pulsing action until blended. Season with salt and pepper.

2. Divide spring greens, chicken, remaining 1 container raspberries and walnuts evenly among 4 plates. Spoon dressing evenly over top.

Makes 4 servings

THAI CHICKEN BROCCOLI SALAD

- 4 ounces uncooked linguine
- Nonstick cooking spray
- ½ pound boneless skinless chicken breasts, cut into strips
- 2 cups broccoli florets
- 2 tablespoons cold water
- ⅔ cup chopped red bell pepper
- 6 green onions, sliced diagonally into 1-inch pieces
- ¼ cup creamy peanut butter
- 2 tablespoons hot water
- 2 tablespoons soy sauce
- 2 teaspoons dark sesame oil
- ½ teaspoon red pepper flakes
- ⅛ teaspoon garlic powder
- ¼ cup unsalted peanuts, chopped

1. Cook pasta according to package directions. Drain; set aside.

2. Spray large nonstick skillet with cooking spray; heat over medium-high heat. Add chicken; stir-fry 5 minutes or until chicken is cooked through. Remove chicken from skillet.

3. Add broccoli and cold water to skillet. Cook, covered, 2 minutes. Uncover; cook and stir 2 minutes or until broccoli is crisp-tender. Remove broccoli from skillet. Combine pasta, chicken, broccoli, bell pepper and green onions in large bowl.

4. Whisk together peanut butter, hot water, soy sauce, oil, pepper flakes and garlic powder in small bowl until well blended. Drizzle over pasta mixture; toss to coat. Sprinkle with peanuts. *Makes 2 servings*

CHICKEN CAESAR SALAD

- 6 ounces chicken tenders
- ¼ cup plus 1 tablespoon Caesar dressing, divided
- Black pepper
- 4 cups (about 5 ounces) prepared Italian salad mix (romaine and radicchio)
- ½ cup croutons
- 2 tablespoons grated Parmesan cheese

1. Cut chicken tenders in half lengthwise and crosswise. Heat 1 tablespoon dressing in large nonstick skillet over medium heat. Add chicken; cook and stir 3 to 4 minutes or until chicken is cooked through. Remove chicken from skillet. Season with pepper; cool slightly.

2. Combine salad mix, croutons, remaining ¼ cup dressing and Parmesan cheese in serving bowl; toss to coat. Top with chicken.

Makes 2 servings

Prep and Cook Time: 20 minutes

MANDARIN CHICKEN SALAD

- ½ cup WISH-BONE® Ranch Dressing
- ¼ cup orange marmalade
- 1¼ pounds boneless, skinless chicken breasts, cooked and sliced (about 3 cups)
- ¼ small red onion, thinly sliced (about ¼ cup)
- 1 package (10 to 12 ounces) mixed salad greens (about 4 cups)
- 1 can (11 ounces) mandarin oranges, drained
- ½ cup seasoned croutons

1. In large bowl, blend dressing and marmalade.

2. Add chicken, red onion and salad greens; toss to coat.

3. Gently fold in oranges and croutons.

Makes 4 servings

Prep Time: 15 minutes

GRILLED CHICKEN SALAD WITH CREAMY TARRAGON DRESSING

- Creamy Tarragon Dressing (recipe follows)
- 1 pound chicken tenders
- 1 teaspoon Cajun seasoning
- 1 package (10 ounces) mixed salad greens
- 2 unpeeled apples, cored and thinly sliced
- 1 cup packed alfalfa sprouts
- 2 tablespoons raisins

1. Spray grid with nonstick cooking spray. Prepare grill for direct cooking.

2. Prepare Creamy Tarragon Dressing; refrigerate until needed. Sprinkle chicken with seasoning.

3. Place chicken on grid. Grill over medium-high heat 5 to 7 minutes on each side or until cooked through.

4. Divide salad greens between 4 plates. Top with chicken, apples and sprouts. Sprinkle with raisins. Serve with dressing.

Makes 4 servings

Prep Time: 10 minutes
Cook Time: 14 minutes

CREAMY TARRAGON DRESSING

- ½ cup plain yogurt
- ¼ cup sour cream
- ¼ cup frozen apple juice concentrate
- 1 tablespoon spicy brown mustard
- 1 tablespoon minced fresh tarragon leaves

Combine all ingredients in small bowl.

Makes about 1 cup

HULA CHICKEN SALAD WITH ORANGE POPPY SEED DRESSING

- ½ cup prepared vinaigrette salad dressing
- ¼ cup *French's*® Honey Dijon Mustard
- 1 tablespoon grated orange peel
- 1 tablespoon water
- 1 teaspoon poppy seeds
- 1 pound chicken tenders
- 1 tablespoon jerk seasoning
- 8 cups cut-up romaine lettuce
- 3 cups cut-up fruit from salad bar, such as oranges, melon, strawberries, pineapple

1. Combine salad dressing, mustard, orange peel, water and poppy seeds; mix well. Reserve.

2. Rub chicken tenders with jerk seasoning. Skewer chicken and grill over medium-high heat until no longer pink, about 5 minutes per side.

3. Arrange lettuce and fruit on salad plates. Top with chicken and serve with dressing.

Makes 4 servings

Prep Time: 15 minutes
Cook Time: 10 minutes

TIP Jerk seasoning is a flavor-packed dry rub used to season meats cooked on the grill. Though it is most commonly associated with the island of Jamaica, it is widely used throughout the Caribbean. Typically, jerk seasoning is a combination of dried chiles, thyme and spices, such as cinnamon, cloves, allspice and ginger.

COUSCOUS CHICKEN SALAD

- ¼ cup plus 1 tablespoon olive oil, divided
- 1 yellow or orange bell pepper, chopped
- 1 small zucchini, chopped
- 1 green onion, finely chopped
- 1 pound chicken tenders, cut into bite-size pieces
- 2 cans (about 14 ounces each) chicken broth
- 10 ounces couscous
- 1 can (about 15 ounces) chickpeas, rinsed and drained
- 1 large tomato, seeded and chopped
- ½ cup chopped fresh cilantro
- ⅓ cup fresh lemon juice
- 1 teaspoon ground cumin
- ¼ teaspoon garlic salt
- Hot pepper sauce

1. Heat 1 tablespoon oil in large skillet over high heat. Add bell pepper, zucchini and green onion; cook and stir 2 minutes or until crisp-tender. Transfer to large bowl.

2. Add chicken and broth to skillet. Bring broth to a boil over high heat. Reduce heat to medium; simmer 4 to 5 minutes or until chicken is cooked through. Remove chicken from broth with slotted spoon. Place in bowl with vegetables; cool.

3. Add couscous to broth. Remove skillet from heat. Cover and let stand 5 minutes or until all liquid is absorbed. Cool 10 minutes.

4. Combine chicken mixture, couscous, chickpeas, tomato and cilantro in large bowl.

5. Whisk together lemon juice, remaining ¼ cup oil, cumin, garlic salt and pepper sauce in small bowl. Pour over couscous mixture; toss to coat. Serve warm or chill 1 hour before serving. *Makes 6 servings*

CARIBBEAN CHICKEN SALAD

- 1½ cups DOLE® Pineapple Juice, divided
- 4 boneless, skinless chicken breast halves
- 1 cup vanilla yogurt
- 3 tablespoons mango chutney or orange marmalade
- 1 teaspoon grated lemon peel
- 1 package (5 to 12 ounces) DOLE® Hearts of Romaine or Italian Salad Blend, or any variety
- 1 pound extra large or jumbo DOLE® Fresh Asparagus, trimmed and cooked
- 2 cups assorted sliced or cut up fruit, such as papaya, kiwi, grapes and melon

• Pour 1 cup pineapple juice in shallow, non-metallic dish. Add chicken; turn to coat both sides. Cover; refrigerate 30 minutes.

• Stir together remaining ½ cup pineapple juice, yogurt, chutney and lemon peel in small bowl; set aside.

• Grill or broil chicken, brushing occasionally with reserved pineapple marinade 5 to 6 minutes on each side or until chicken is no longer pink in center. Discard remaining marinade. Slice chicken diagonally.

• Arrange chicken on four dinner plates lined with salad greens. Evenly divide asparagus and fruit on plates. Serve with pineapple yogurt dressing. *Makes 4 servings*

Microwave Directions for Asparagus: Place asparagus in microwave-safe dish with 2 tablespoons water. Microwave on HIGH 5 to 7 minutes or until tender-crisp; stirring once during heating.

Prep Time: 15 minutes
Marinate Time: 30 minutes
Grill Time: 10 minutes

CHICKEN AND APPLE SPRING GREENS WITH POPPY SEEDS

1 package (5 ounces) spring greens
12 ounces cooked chicken strips
1 large Golden Delicious apple, unpeeled, thinly sliced
⅓ cup thinly sliced red onion
1 ounce crumbled goat cheese (optional)
¼ cup cider vinegar
2 tablespoons sugar
2 tablespoons canola oil
½ teaspoon poppy seeds
¼ teaspoon salt
⅛ teaspoon red pepper flakes

1. Arrange equal amounts spring greens, chicken, apple and onion on each of 4 plates. Sprinkle with goat cheese, if desired.

2. Whisk vinegar, sugar, oil, poppy seeds, salt and pepper flakes in small bowl until well blended. Spoon dressing over salads.

Makes 2 to 3 servings

MEDITERRANEAN CHICKEN PASTA SALAD

8 ounces whole wheat rotini pasta
1 jar (6 ounces) marinated artichoke hearts
¾ pound boneless skinless chicken breast, cut into 1-inch pieces
Black pepper
⅓ cup fresh lemon juice
2 tablespoons Greek seasoning
1 tablespoon olive oil
1 cup roasted red peppers, drained and chopped
½ cup crumbled feta cheese

1. Cook pasta according to package directions; drain. Rinse under cold running water; drain well. Place in large bowl. Drain artichoke hearts, reserving marinade. Chop artichoke hearts; add to pasta.

2. Heat 1 tablespoon reserved artichoke marinade in large skillet over medium-high heat. Add chicken; season with black pepper. Cook and stir 3 to 4 minutes or until chicken is cooked through. Add to pasta.

3. Whisk together remaining artichoke marinade, lemon juice, seasoning and oil in small bowl. Add roasted peppers, cheese and marinade mixture to pasta mixture; toss to combine. Cover and refrigerate 2 hours.

Makes 4 servings

CITRUS SALAD RIO GRANDE

1 large red bell pepper
4 corn tortillas
1 tablespoon corn oil
Salt
4 boneless, skinless chicken breast halves
3 teaspoons Mexican seasoning*
2 tablespoons olive oil
6 cups mixed torn salad greens
2 Texas Red Grapefruit, peeled and sectioned
2 scallions, thinly sliced
Creamy Rio Grande Dressing (recipe follows)

**A combination of seasonings can be substituted for the Mexican seasoning. Combine 1 teaspoon each of garlic salt, cumin and chili powder with ½ teaspoon dried oregano.*

To roast pepper, place on baking sheet and roast under broiler, turning occasionally, until skin is blistered on all sides. Remove from oven. Cover with damp paper towel. When cool enough to handle, peel off skin. Cut off stem; remove seeds and membrane. Thinly slice pepper; set aside or refrigerate for longer storage.

To prepare tortilla crisps, use kitchen shears to cut tortillas into ¼-inch strips. Brush rimmed baking sheet with 1 tablespoon corn oil and spread strips in a single layer. Bake at 400°F about 8 to 10 minutes or until golden brown, turning halfway through cooking. Remove from oven; season with salt. Set aside.

When ready to cook chicken, pound to ½-inch thickness. In small bowl, combine Mexican seasoning with olive oil. Brush mixture over chicken and grill or broil 6 to 8 inches from heat source. Cook 10 to 18 minutes or until cooked through, turning 2 to 3 times and basting with additional seasoned oil if needed. Remove from heat and cut into strips.

Arrange greens on 4 individual plates or on large serving platter; top with chicken, red pepper and grapefruit. Garnish with tortilla crisps and scallions. Serve with Creamy Rio Grande Dressing.

Makes 4 servings

Note: The roasted red pepper, tortilla crisps and Creamy Rio Grande Dressing can be prepared a day in advance, if desired.

Favorite recipe from **TexaSweet Citrus Marketing, Inc.**

CREAMY RIO GRANDE DRESSING

- ½ cup plain yogurt
- ½ cup mayonnaise
- ⅓ cup cilantro sprigs
- 1 clove garlic
- ½ teaspoon chili powder
- ¼ teaspoon ground cumin
- ¼ teaspoon salt

In a blender, combine all the dressing ingredients; whirl until blended.

Makes about 1 cup

Favorite recipe from TexaSweet Citrus Marketing, Inc.

CHICKEN AND BLACK BEAN SALAD

- 2 tablespoons vegetable oil, divided
- 1 medium red onion, diced
- 1 pound boneless skinless chicken breasts, cut into ¾-inch pieces
- 1 can (16 ounces) black beans, drained and rinsed
- 1 medium tomato, diced
- ½ cup peperoncini peppers, seeded and diced
- 3 tablespoons chopped fresh parsley
- 2 tablespoons cider vinegar
- 1 teaspoon salt
- 1 teaspoon Original TABASCO® brand Pepper Sauce
- Lettuce leaves
- Whole pickled peppers for garnish

Heat 1 tablespoon oil in 10-inch skillet over medium heat until hot. Add red onion; cook until tender, about 5 minutes, stirring occasionally. Remove to large bowl. In same skillet add remaining 1 tablespoon oil. Over medium-high heat cook chicken pieces until well browned on all sides, about 5 minutes, stirring occasionally.

In large bowl toss red onion with chicken, beans, tomato, diced peperoncini peppers, parsley, vinegar, salt and TABASCO® Sauce to mix well.

To serve, line large platter with lettuce leaves; top with chicken salad. Garnish with pickled peppers.

Makes 4 servings

CHICKEN STIR–FRY SALAD WITH PEANUT DRESSING

- ½ cup chicken broth or water
- ½ cup smooth peanut butter
- 2 tablespoons fresh lime or lemon juice
- 2 tablespoons molasses or brown sugar
- 1 tablespoon soy sauce
- ¼ teaspoon ground red pepper
- ⅛ teaspoon garlic powder
- 1 pound chicken tenders, cut into ½-inch pieces
- ¼ teaspoon salt
- 2 tablespoons vegetable oil
- 1 package (16 ounces) frozen broccoli, carrots and water chestnuts mix
- 2 tablespoons soy sauce
- 1 package (10 ounces) salad greens
- ¼ cup dry roasted peanuts

1. For Peanut Dressing, microwave broth on HIGH 30 seconds or until hot. Place in blender with peanut butter, lime juice, molasses, soy sauce, red pepper and garlic powder; process 15 seconds or until well blended.

2. Sprinkle chicken with salt. Heat oil in wok or large deep skillet over medium-high heat. Add chicken; stir-fry 3 minutes or until chicken begins to brown.

3. Add vegetables. Reduce heat to medium. Cover and cook 5 minutes or until chicken is cooked through and vegetables are crisp-tender, stirring occasionally. Stir in soy sauce. Remove from heat.

4. Arrange salad greens on plates; top with chicken mixture. Sprinkle with peanuts. Serve with Peanut Dressing.

Makes 4 servings

CHICKEN AND CANTALOUPE SALAD WITH TOASTED PECANS

- ½ cup mayonnaise
- 1 tablespoon cider vinegar
- 1 tablespoon honey
- ½ teaspoon curry powder
- ¼ teaspoon ground ginger
- 4 cups shredded cooked chicken
- 1 cup thinly sliced celery
- ¼ cup thinly sliced red onion
- 1 small cantaloupe
- ½ cup toasted pecan halves, divided
- 6 cups Romaine or Boston lettuce leaves

1. For dressing, whisk together mayonnaise, vinegar, honey, curry powder and ginger in small bowl.

2. Combine chicken, celery and onion in medium bowl. Add dressing; toss to coat.

3. Peel and seed cantaloupe; cut half into small cubes and half into 8 wedges for garnish. Add cantaloupe cubes and ¼ cup pecans to salad; toss to mix.

4. Line plates with lettuce leaves; top with chicken mixture. Garnish with cantaloupe wedges and sprinkle with remaining pecans.

Makes 4 servings

WILD THYME SUMMER SALAD

- 3 cups cooked rice
- 2 boneless, skinless chicken breasts, cooked and cut into 1-inch cubes
- 1 (8½-ounce) jar sun-dried tomatoes, drained and chopped
- ⅓ cup chopped Kalamata olives
- ½ cup prepared vinaigrette
- ¼ cup chopped fresh thyme leaves

In large bowl, combine rice, chicken, tomatoes, olives, vinaigrette and thyme. Toss well.

Makes 4 servings

Favorite recipe from USA Rice

SOUTHWEST CHICKEN SALAD

- 1 cup plus 2 tablespoons ORTEGA® Taco Sauce
- 1½ pounds boneless skinless chicken breasts
- Juice of ½ lime
- 3 tablespoons mayonnaise
- 3 tablespoons olive oil
- 1 teaspoon Worcestershire sauce
- ½ teaspoon POLANER® Chopped Garlic
- 1 head iceberg lettuce, chopped
- 1 bag (10 ounces) mixed greens
- 1 cup shredded taco cheese blend
- 6 ORTEGA® Yellow Corn Taco Shells, broken into small pieces

Pour 1 cup taco sauce over chicken breasts in shallow pan. Cover; marinate 15 minutes in refrigerator. Turn chicken breasts over and marinate in refrigerator 15 minutes longer.

Preheat grill until piping hot, about 15 minutes. Place chicken breasts on grill and cook 5 minutes. Turn over and cook another 5 minutes, until chicken is cooked through. Remove from grill; squeeze lime juice over chicken breasts and slice into strips.

For dressing, whisk mayonnaise, oil, Worcestershire sauce, garlic and remaining 2 tablespoons taco sauce in small bowl (if dressing is too thick, add more olive oil). Toss dressing in large bowl with lettuce and mixed greens. Divide mixture among serving plates. Top evenly with sliced chicken. Sprinkle with cheese and broken taco shells.

Makes 6 servings

Prep Time: 5 minutes
Start-to-Finish Time: 45 minutes

TIP Worcestershire sauce is a savory sauce developed in India and named after the English town, Worcester, where it was first bottled. It has a complex and unique flavor and is used as a seasoning in soups, salad dressings and marinades.

CURRIED CHICKEN & ZUCCHINI SALAD

- ½ cup plain yogurt
- ⅓ cup mayonnaise
- 2 tablespoons chili sauce
- 1 teaspoon white wine vinegar
- 1 teaspoon diced shallot or onion
- ¾ teaspoon curry powder
- ¼ teaspoon salt
- 2 cups shredded cooked chicken
- 1 cup seedless red grapes
- 1 medium zucchini, cut into matchstick-size strips
- Leaf lettuce
- ¼ cup slivered almonds, toasted*

**To toast almonds, spread in single layer in small skillet. Heat over medium-high heat 3 to 5 minutes or until golden brown, stirring frequently.*

1. Combine yogurt, mayonnaise, chili sauce, vinegar, shallot, curry powder and salt in large bowl; stir until smooth. Add chicken, grapes and zucchini; toss to coat.

2. Arrange lettuce on plates. Top with chicken mixture; sprinkle with almonds. *Makes 2 servings*

CHICKEN SALAD WITH FENNEL AND WALNUTS

- 6 chicken thighs, skinned
- 1 stalk fresh fennel (about ½ pound)
- 4 to 5 tablespoons mayonnaise
- 1 teaspoon chopped fresh chives
- 3 tablespoons walnuts, toasted and chopped
- Salt and black pepper to taste

Cut off tall stalks and feathery leaves from fennel bulb; rinse well and cut in half. Reserve 2 tablespoons minced fennel leaves. Trim base from fennel bulb; remove tough outer layers. Slice fennel hearts crosswise to form celery-like pieces. Measure ½ cup; set aside. Place chicken, fennel stalks and remaining leaves in a large pot; cover with water. Bring to a boil; skim the top. Reduce heat and simmer 25 minutes or until done. Remove chicken from the broth; cool partially. Pull meat from the bones; cut into small chunks. In a medium bowl combine mayonnaise, reserved minced fennel leaves and chives. Mix in chicken, sliced fennel and walnuts. Season with salt and pepper. *Makes 4 servings*

Favorite recipe from **National Chicken Council**

BUFFALO CHICKEN SALAD ITALIANO

- ½ cup *Frank's® RedHot®* Buffalo Wing Sauce
- ½ cup prepared Italian salad dressing
- 1 pound frozen chicken tenders, thawed
- 8 cups torn salad greens
- 1 cup sliced celery
- 1 cup crumbled Gorgonzola or blue cheese

1. Combine Wing Sauce and salad dressing in bowl. Pour ½ cup mixture over chicken tenders in large bowl. Cover and refrigerate 20 minutes.

2. Cook chicken on electric grill pan or barbecue grill for 3 to 5 minutes until no longer pink in center.

3. Arrange salad greens, celery and cheese on serving plates. Top with chicken and drizzle with remaining Wing Sauce mixture. *Makes 4 servings*

Tip: You may substitute 1 pound boneless skinless chicken breast halves for chicken tenders.

Prep Time: 5 minutes
Marinate Time: 20 minutes
Cook Time: 5 minutes

MANGO CHICKEN SALAD

- ¼ cup (plus 2 tablespoons) plain yogurt
- ¼ cup chopped fresh cilantro
- 1 tablespoon mango chutney (optional)
- 1 tablespoon fresh lime juice
- 1 teaspoon Dijon mustard
- ½ teaspoon ground turmeric
- ⅛ teaspoon ground red pepper
- Salt and black pepper
- 1 cup shredded cooked chicken
- ½ ripe mango, peeled, seeded and diced
- 5 ounces baby spinach
- ¼ cup shredded coconut

Whisk together yogurt, cilantro, mango chutney, if desired, lime juice, mustard, turmeric and red pepper in large bowl. Season with salt and black pepper. Add chicken and mango; toss well. Serve over spinach; sprinkle with coconut. *Makes 2 servings*

CHINESE CHICKEN SALAD

4 cups chopped bok choy
3 cups diced cooked chicken
1 cup shredded carrots
2 tablespoons minced fresh chives or green onion
2 tablespoons chili garlic sauce*
1½ tablespoons peanut or canola oil
1 tablespoon balsamic vinegar
1 tablespoon soy sauce
1 teaspoon minced fresh ginger

**Chili garlic sauce is available in the Asian foods section of most supermarkets.*

1. Place bok choy, chicken, carrots and chives in large bowl.

2. Combine chili garlic sauce, oil, vinegar, soy sauce and ginger in small bowl; mix well. Pour over chicken mixture; toss gently. *Makes 4 servings*

DIJON ROASTED CHICKEN SALAD

2 tablespoons Dijon mustard
2 tablespoons red wine vinegar
3 tablespoons olive oil
1 teaspoon chopped thyme
½ teaspoon kosher salt
⅛ teaspoon ground black pepper
1 pound roasted chicken, pulled into 1-inch pieces
8 ounces Yukon Gold potatoes, quartered and boiled
6 ounces green beans, blanched
1 cup California Ripe Olives, whole, pitted
1 cup wedged radishes
8 ounces butter lettuce, washed and torn

In a large mixing bowl, whisk together mustard and vinegar. Continue whisking and pour in oil in a steady stream until fully emulsified, then whisk in thyme, salt and pepper. Toss chicken, potatoes, green beans, California Ripe Olives, radishes and lettuce with dressing until evenly coated. Serve immediately. *Makes 4 servings*

Favorite recipe from **California Olive Industry**

LIGHT & EASY CHICKEN SALAD

½ cup low-fat Italian salad dressing
¼ cup *French's*® Spicy Brown Mustard
¼ cup orange juice
1 teaspoon grated orange peel
3 cups (12 ounces) sliced cooked chicken
1½ cups frozen whole green beans, thawed
½ pound red potatoes, cooked and cut into ½-inch wedges
½ cup sliced celery
½ cup sliced red onion

1. Whisk together salad dressing, mustard, orange juice and peel in large bowl. Add chicken and vegetables; toss gently until evenly coated. Season to taste with salt and pepper.

2. Cover; chill in refrigerator 30 minutes. Serve over salad greens or in sandwiches, as desired.

Makes 6 servings

GRILLED CHICKEN TOSTADA SALAD

1 pound boneless skinless chicken breast halves
¾ cup *Frank's*® *RedHot*® *Chile 'n Lime*™ Hot Sauce, divided
2 teaspoons chili powder
4 cups tortilla chips
8 cups shredded iceberg lettuce
1 cup shredded Cheddar cheese
1 cup salsa
1 cup canned or thawed frozen whole kernel corn
½ cup sliced Spanish olives

1. Place chicken and ½ cup *Chile 'n Lime*™ Hot Sauce in plastic bag. Refrigerate 20 minutes.

2. Grill chicken 10 minutes or until no longer pink in center. Slice chicken and toss with remaining *Chile 'n Lime*™ Hot Sauce and chili powder.

3. Place 1 cup tortilla chips in each salad bowl. Layer remaining ingredients and chicken on top, dividing evenly among bowls. If desired, garnish with sour cream and chopped cilantro.

Makes 4 servings

SPICY SQUASH & CHICKEN SOUP

- 1 tablespoon vegetable oil
- 1 small onion, finely chopped
- 1 stalk celery, finely chopped
- 1 small delicata or butternut squash, peeled and cut into 1-inch cubes
- 2 cups chicken broth
- 1 can (about 14 ounces) diced tomatoes with chiles
- 1 cup chopped cooked chicken
- ½ teaspoon ground ginger
- ⅛ teaspoon ground cumin
- 2 teaspoons fresh lime juice
- Salt and black pepper
- 1 tablespoon minced fresh cilantro (optional)

1. Heat oil in large saucepan over medium heat. Add onion and celery; cook and stir 5 minutes or until just tender. Add squash, broth, tomatoes, chicken, ginger and cumin; mix well.

2. Reduce heat to low. Cover and cook 30 minutes or until squash is tender. Stir in lime juice. Season with salt and pepper. Sprinkle with cilantro, if desired.

Makes 4 servings

CHICKEN AND BLACK BEAN CHILI

- 1 pound boneless skinless chicken thighs, cut into 1-inch pieces
- 2 teaspoons ground cumin
- 2 teaspoons chili powder
- ¾ teaspoon salt
- 1 green bell pepper, diced
- 1 small onion, chopped
- 3 cloves garlic, minced
- 1 can (about 14 ounces) diced tomatoes
- 1 cup chunky salsa
- 1 can (about 15 ounces) black beans, rinsed and drained

Slow Cooker Directions

1. Combine chicken, cumin, chili powder and salt in slow cooker; toss to coat.

2. Add bell pepper, onion and garlic; mix well. Stir in tomatoes and salsa. Cover; cook on LOW 5 to 6 hours or on HIGH 2½ to 3 hours or until chicken is tender.

3. Increase heat to HIGH; stir in beans. Cover; cook 5 to 10 minutes or until beans are heated through.

Makes 4 servings

CALICO MINESTRONE SOUP

- 2 cans (14 ounces each) chicken broth
- ¼ cup uncooked small shell pasta
- 1 can (14½ ounces) DEL MONTE® Stewed Tomatoes - Italian Recipe
- 1 can (8¾ ounces) *or* 1 cup kidney beans, drained
- ½ cup chopped cooked chicken or beef
- 1 carrot, cubed
- 1 stalk celery, sliced
- ½ teaspoon dried basil, crushed

1. Bring broth to boil in large saucepan; stir in pasta and boil 5 minutes.

2. Add remaining ingredients.

3. Reduce heat; cover and simmer 20 minutes. Garnish with grated Parmesan cheese, if desired.

Makes about 6 servings

• CHICKEN AND BLACK BEAN CHILI •

THYME FOR CHICKEN STEW WITH POLENTA DUMPLINGS

- 4 tablespoons olive oil, divided
- 2 pounds boneless skinless chicken thighs
- 2 medium eggplants, chopped
- 4 tomatoes, seeded and diced
- 2 large onions, chopped
- 1 cup chicken broth
- ⅓ cup pitted black olives, sliced
- 1 tablespoon chopped fresh thyme *or* 1 teaspoon dried thyme
- 1 tablespoon red wine vinegar
- Polenta Dumplings (recipe follows)

1. Preheat oven to 350°F.

2. Heat 1 tablespoon oil in Dutch oven over medium-high heat. Cook chicken in batches 4 to 5 minutes or until browned on all sides. Remove and set aside.

3. Heat remaining 3 tablespoons oil in same Dutch oven; add eggplants, tomatoes and onions. Reduce heat to medium. Cook 5 minutes, stirring occasionally. Return chicken to Dutch oven. Add broth, olives, thyme and vinegar; stir to combine. Bring to a boil. Transfer to oven; cover and bake 1 hour. Meanwhile, prepare Polenta Dumplings.

4. Remove stew from oven; top with rounded tablespoonfuls dumpling mixture. Bake, uncovered, 20 minutes or until dumplings are cooked through.

Makes 6 servings

POLENTA DUMPLINGS

- 3½ cups chicken broth
- 1 cup polenta or yellow cornmeal
- 1 egg, beaten
- ½ cup grated Parmesan cheese
- ¼ cup chopped fresh parsley
- 2 tablespoons butter

1. Bring broth to a boil in medium saucepan over medium-high heat. Gradually whisk in polenta. Reduce heat to low; simmer 15 minutes or until thickened, stirring constantly.

2. Remove saucepan from heat; stir in egg, Parmesan cheese, parsley and butter.

Makes 6 servings

SIMMERING HOT & SOUR SOUP

2 cans (about 14 ounces each) chicken broth
1 cup chopped cooked chicken
4 ounces shiitake mushroom caps, thinly sliced
½ cup sliced bamboo shoots, cut into thin strips
3 tablespoons rice wine vinegar
2 tablespoons soy sauce
1 teaspoon hot chili oil
4 ounces firm tofu, well drained and cut into ½-inch pieces
2 teaspoons dark sesame oil
2 tablespoons water
2 tablespoons cornstarch
Chopped fresh cilantro or sliced green onions (optional)

Slow Cooker Directions

1. Combine broth, chicken, mushrooms, bamboo shoots, vinegar, soy sauce and chili oil in 4-quart slow cooker. Cover; cook on LOW 3 to 4 hours.

2. Stir in tofu and sesame oil. Blend water into cornstarch in small bowl until smooth. Stir into slow cooker. Cover; cook on HIGH 15 minutes or until thickened. Garnish with cilantro. *Makes 4 servings*

CHIPOTLE CHICKEN NOODLE SOUP

2 tablespoons olive oil
1 medium yellow onion, finely chopped
4 cloves garlic, minced
½ pound boneless, skinless chicken breast, cut into bite-size pieces
3 cups water
3 cubes HERB-OX® chicken flavored bouillon
1 chipotle pepper in adobo sauce, chopped
1 cup frozen egg noodles
1 cup fresh diced tomatoes
1 to 2 teaspoons sugar

In large saucepan, in oil, cook onion and garlic until tender. Add chicken and sauté for 2 to 3 minutes. Add water, bouillon, chipotle pepper and noodles. Reduce heat and simmer for 15 to 20 minutes or until noodles are tender. Stir in tomatoes and sugar. *Makes 4 servings*

• SIMMERING HOT & SOUR SOUP •

COCONUT CURRY CHICKEN SOUP

- 3 cups chicken broth
- 8 boneless skinless chicken thighs
- 1 cup chopped onion, divided
- 1 teaspoon salt, divided
- 4 whole cloves
- 1 tablespoon butter
- 2 tablespoons curry powder
- 1¼ cups coconut milk
- 3 tablespoons crystallized ginger, minced
- ¼ cup plus 1 tablespoon chopped fresh mint, divided
- ¼ teaspoon ground cloves
- 1½ cups half-and-half
- 3 cups cooked rice
- Lime wedges (optional)

1. Bring broth to a boil in large skillet over high heat. Add chicken, ½ cup onion, ½ teaspoon salt and whole cloves. Return to a boil. Reduce heat; cover and simmer 40 minutes or until chicken is very tender.

2. Remove chicken; set aside. Reserve 1 cup broth, discarding remainder of cooking liquid, onion and cloves. Increase heat to medium-high; melt butter in skillet. Add remaining ½ cup onion; cook and stir about 4 minutes or until translucent. Sprinkle curry powder over onions; cook and stir 20 seconds or just until fragrant.

3. Add coconut milk, ginger, 1 tablespoon mint, ground cloves and reserved 1 cup broth to skillet; cover and simmer 10 minutes. Add chicken to coconut mixture; cover and simmer 15 minutes. Stir in half-and-half and remaining ½ teaspoon salt. Shred chicken slightly with fork. Cook 1 minute or until heated through. Sprinkle with remaining ¼ cup mint. Serve with rice and lime wedges, if desired. *Makes 4 servings*

TIP Crystallized (or candied) ginger has been cooked in a sugar syrup and coated with coarse sugar. It can be found either in the ethnic or baking sections of large supermarkets as well as in specialty markets. Its sharp, sweet flavor makes it ideal for both sweet and savory dishes, as well as eating alone as a candy.

HEARTY CHICKEN CHILI

- 1 medium onion, finely chopped
- 1 jalapeño pepper,* seeded and minced
- 1 clove garlic, minced
- 1½ teaspoons chili powder
- ¾ teaspoon salt
- ½ teaspoon ground cumin
- ½ teaspoon dried oregano
- ½ teaspoon black pepper
- 2 cans (about 15 ounces each) hominy, rinsed and drained
- 1 can (about 15 ounces) pinto beans, rinsed and drained
- 1½ pounds boneless skinless chicken thighs, cut into 1-inch pieces
- 1 cup chicken broth
- 1 tablespoon all-purpose flour
- Chopped fresh cilantro (optional)

**Jalapeño peppers can sting and irritate the skin, so wear rubber gloves when handling peppers and do not touch eyes.*

Slow Cooker Directions

1. Combine onion, jalapeño pepper, garlic, chili powder, salt, cumin, oregano and black pepper in 5-quart slow cooker.

2. Add hominy, beans, chicken and broth; stir well to combine. Cover; cook on LOW 7 hours.

3. Combine flour and 3 tablespoons cooking liquid in small bowl. Add to slow cooker. Cover; cook on HIGH 10 minutes or until thickened. Sprinkle with cilantro before serving, if desired.

Makes 6 servings

Prep Time: 15 minutes
Cook Time: 7 hours (LOW), plus 10 minutes (HIGH)

ACORN SQUASH SOUP WITH CHICKEN AND RED PEPPER MEATBALLS

½ medium acorn squash (about ¾ pound)
½ pound ground chicken
1 red bell pepper, finely chopped
1 egg, lightly beaten
1 teaspoon dried parsley flakes
1 teaspoon ground coriander
¼ teaspoon ground cinnamon
½ teaspoon black pepper
3 cups vegetable broth
Sour cream (optional)
Ground red pepper (optional)

1. Pierce squash skin with fork. Place in microwaveable dish; microwave on HIGH 8 to 10 minutes or until tender. Cool 10 minutes.

2. Combine chicken, bell pepper, egg, parsley flakes, coriander, cinnamon and black pepper in medium bowl. Form meatballs and place in microwaveable dish. Microwave on HIGH 5 minutes or until cooked through.

3. Scoop seeds out of cooled squash; discard. Scrape squash flesh into small saucepan; discard shell. Mash squash with potato masher. Add broth and meatballs; cook over medium-high heat 12 minutes, stirring occasionally.

4. Top with sour cream and sprinkle with red pepper, if desired.

Makes 2 servings

COCONUT CHICKEN CHOWDER

2 tablespoons vegetable oil, divided
1 pound boneless, skinless chicken breasts, cut into bite-size pieces
1 large stalk celery, sliced
1 red bell pepper, seeded and diced
1 large green onion, thinly sliced
1 large clove garlic, minced
1 (14-ounce) can coconut milk
½ cup water
¼ cup creamy peanut butter
2 teaspoons Original TABASCO® brand Pepper Sauce
1¼ teaspoons salt
Chopped fresh cilantro (optional)

Heat 1 tablespoon oil in 3-quart saucepan over medium-high heat. Add chicken pieces; cook 5 to 10 minutes or until lightly browned on all sides, stirring frequently. Remove chicken to plate with slotted spoon. Add remaining 1 tablespoon oil to saucepan; cook celery and red bell pepper 5 minutes over medium heat. Add green onion and garlic; cook 1 minute.

Return chicken to saucepan; add coconut milk, water, peanut butter, TABASCO® Sauce and salt. Heat to boiling over high heat. Reduce heat to low; cover and simmer 10 minutes, stirring occasionally. Garnish with cilantro, if desired. *Makes 4 servings*

Note: Coconut milk is readily available in the ethnic section of large supermarkets. Be sure to purchase unsweetened coconut milk rather than "cream of coconut," used mainly for desserts and mixed drinks.

CAJUN–STYLE CHICKEN SOUP

- 1½ pounds chicken thighs
- 4 cups chicken broth
- 1 can (8 ounces) tomato sauce
- 1 medium onion, chopped
- 2 stalks celery, sliced
- 2 cloves garlic, minced
- 2 bay leaves
- 1 teaspoon salt
- ½ teaspoon ground cumin
- ¼ teaspoon paprika
- ¼ teaspoon ground red pepper
- ¼ teaspoon black pepper
- Dash white pepper
- 1 green bell pepper, chopped
- ⅓ cup uncooked rice
- 8 ounces fresh or frozen okra, cut into ½-inch slices
- Hot pepper sauce (optional)

1. Combine chicken, broth, tomato sauce, onion, celery, garlic, bay leaves, salt, cumin, paprika, red pepper, black pepper and white pepper in 5-quart Dutch oven. Bring to a boil over high heat. Reduce heat to medium-low; simmer 1 hour or until chicken is tender. Skim off any foam that rises to the surface.

2. Remove chicken; cool slightly. Remove chicken meat from bones; discard skin and bones. Cut chicken into bite-size pieces.

3. Add chicken, bell pepper and rice to soup. Bring to a boil over high heat. Reduce heat to medium-low; simmer 12 minutes or until rice is tender. Add okra; simmer 8 minutes or until tender. Discard bay leaves. Serve with hot pepper sauce, if desired. *Makes 6 servings*

MIDDLE EASTERN CHICKEN SOUP

- 2½ cups water
- 1 can (about 15 ounces) chickpeas, rinsed and drained
- 1 can (about 14 ounces) chicken broth
- 1 cup chopped cooked chicken
- 1 small onion, chopped
- 1 carrot, chopped
- 1 clove garlic, minced
- 1 teaspoon dried oregano
- 1 teaspoon ground cumin
- ½ (10-ounce) package spinach leaves, stemmed and coarsely chopped

Combine water, chickpeas, broth, chicken, onion, carrot, garlic, oregano, and cumin in medium saucepan. Bring to boil over high heat. Reduce heat and simmer, covered, 15 minutes. Stir in spinach; simmer, uncovered, 2 minutes or until spinach wilts. *Makes 4 servings*

MULLIGATAWNY VEG•ALL® SOUP

- 1 tablespoon butter or olive oil
- 1 cup (5 ounces) chopped yellow onion
- ½ cup (about 2 ounces) chopped celery
- ½ cup chopped green bell pepper
- 1 cup (4 ounces) peeled, seeded and chopped tart apple
- 1 tablespoon curry powder
- 6 cups chicken broth
- ½ cup uncooked long-grain white rice
- 8 ounces chicken breast meat, cut in ½-inch chunks
- 1 can (15 ounces) VEG•ALL® Original Mixed Vegetables, drained
- ½ cup coconut milk or heavy cream
- Salt and pepper to taste

In medium pot, heat butter or oil over medium heat and cook onions until soft but not brown. Add celery, bell pepper and apple; stir well. Add curry powder, stir for a minute, then add broth. Bring to a boil and add rice. Stir well and reduce heat. Simmer 10 minutes, then add chicken and Veg•All. Simmer 10 minutes longer. Add coconut milk or cream and stir well. Season with salt and pepper. *Makes 8 servings*

Cook's Tip: If you are using cream and the soup is not slightly sweet, add ¼ to ½ teaspoon of sugar before serving.

CREAMY FARMHOUSE CHICKEN AND GARDEN SOUP

- ½ package (16 ounces) frozen pepper stir-fry mix
- 1 cup frozen corn
- 1 medium zucchini, sliced
- 4 chicken thighs, skinned
- 1 can (about 14 ounces) chicken broth
- ½ teaspoon minced garlic
- ½ teaspoon dried thyme
- 2 ounces uncooked egg noodles
- 1 cup half-and-half
- ½ cup frozen green peas
- 2 tablespoons chopped fresh parsley
- 2 tablespoons butter
- 1 teaspoon salt
- ½ teaspoon coarsely ground black pepper

Slow Cooker Directions

1. Coat 4-quart slow cooker with nonstick cooking spray. Place stir-fry mix, corn and zucchini in slow cooker; top with chicken, broth, garlic and thyme. Cover; cook on HIGH 3 to 4 hours or until chicken is cooked through and tender. Remove chicken; set aside to cool slightly.

2. Add noodles to slow cooker. Cover; cook 20 minutes or until noodles are done.

3. Meanwhile, debone and chop chicken. Return to slow cooker. Stir in half-and-half, peas, parsley, butter, salt and black pepper. Let stand 5 minutes before serving. *Makes 4 servings*

Note: To skin chicken easily, grasp skin with paper towel and pull away. Repeat with fresh paper towel for each piece of chicken, discarding skins and towels.

Prep Time: 15 minutes
Cook Time: about 3 to 4 hours

CHUNKY CHICKEN AND VEGETABLE SOUP

- 1 tablespoon canola oil
- ½ pound boneless skinless chicken breasts, diced
- ½ cup chopped green bell pepper
- ½ cup thinly sliced celery
- 2 green onions, sliced
- 2 cans (about 14 ounces each) chicken broth
- 1 cup water
- ½ cup sliced carrots
- 2 tablespoons whipping cream
- 1 tablespoon finely chopped fresh parsley (optional)
- ¼ teaspoon dried thyme
- ⅛ teaspoon black pepper

1. Heat oil in large saucepan over medium heat. Add chicken; cook and stir 4 to 5 minutes or until cooked through. Add bell pepper, celery and green onions. Cook and stir 7 minutes or until vegetables are tender.

2. Add broth, water, carrots, cream, parsley, if desired, thyme and black pepper. Simmer 10 minutes or until carrots are tender. *Makes 4 servings*

HEAD–'EM–OFF–AT–THE–PASS WHITE CHILI

- 1 tablespoon olive oil
- ½ cup chopped onion
- 2 cans (15 ounces each) cannellini beans, undrained
- 1 jar (11 ounces) NEWMAN'S OWN® Bandito Salsa, divided
- 1½ cups chopped cooked chicken
- ½ cup chicken broth
- 1 teaspoon oregano leaves
- ½ teaspoon celery salt
- 1½ cups (6 ounces) shredded mozzarella cheese, divided

Heat oil in 2-quart saucepan; add onion and cook and stir until tender. Stir in beans, ½ cup of Newman's Own® Bandito Salsa, chicken, chicken broth, oregano and celery salt. Cover; simmer over medium heat 10 minutes, stirring occasionally. Just before serving, stir in 1 cup of mozzarella cheese. Divide chili evenly among serving bowls. Top each with a portion of remaining mozzarella and salsa. *Makes 4 servings*

CHICKEN AND SAUSAGE GUMBO WITH BEER

- ½ cup all-purpose flour
- ½ cup vegetable oil
- 4½ cups chicken broth
- 1 bottle (12 ounces) beer
- 3 pounds boneless skinless chicken thighs
- 1½ teaspoons salt, divided
- ¾ teaspoon ground red pepper, divided
- ½ teaspoon garlic powder
- 1 pound fully cooked andouille sausage, sliced into rounds
- 1 large onion, chopped
- ½ red bell pepper, chopped
- ½ green bell pepper, chopped
- 2 stalks celery, chopped
- 2 cloves garlic, minced
- 2 bay leaves
- ½ teaspoon black pepper
- 1 teaspoon filé powder (optional)
- 3 cups hot cooked rice
- ½ cup sliced green onions (optional)

1. Stir together flour and oil In large saucepan or Dutch oven. Cook over medium-low heat 1 hour or until mixture is the color of milk chocolate, stirring frequently. (Once mixture begins to darken, watch carefully to avoid burning.)

2. Meanwhile, bring broth and beer to simmer in medium saucepan over medium heat. Keep warm over low heat. Season chicken with ½ teaspoon salt, ¼ teaspoon red pepper and garlic powder.

3. Ladle in warm broth mixture, whisking between additions to break up lumps. Add chicken, sausage, onion, bell peppers, celery, garlic, bay leaves, black pepper, filé powder, if desired, remaining 1 teaspoon salt and ½ teaspoon red pepper; stir well. Bring to a simmer. Cover and simmer over low heat 1 to 2 hours. Remove and discard bay leaves. Serve gumbo over rice. Garnish with green onions. *Makes 6 servings*

SPINACH NOODLE BOWL WITH GINGER

- 1 can (48 ounces) chicken broth (about 6 cups)
- 4 ounces uncooked vermicelli noodles, broken into thirds
- 1½ cups shredded carrots
- 3 ounces snow peas, cut in half, stems removed
- 4 cups packed spinach leaves (4 ounces)
- 1½ cups diced cooked chicken or shrimp
- ½ cup finely chopped green onions
- 1 tablespoon grated fresh ginger
- 1 teaspoon soy sauce (optional)
- ⅛ to ¼ teaspoon red pepper flakes

1. Bring broth to a boil in Dutch oven over high heat. Add vermicelli; return to a boil. Cook until just tender (about 2 minutes less than package instructions). Add carrots and snow peas; cook 2 minutes or until pasta is tender.

2. Remove from heat; stir in spinach, chicken, green onions, ginger, soy sauce, if desired, and pepper flakes. Let stand 2 minutes to before serving.

Makes 4 servings

TIP Look for diced cooked chicken in the refrigerated meat section of your supermarket or use leftover chicken from another meal. Prepared rotisserie chickens are also a good time-saving option.

TUSCAN CHICKEN WITH WHITE BEANS

- 1 large bulb fennel (about ¾ pound)
- 1 teaspoon olive oil
- 1 teaspoon dried rosemary
- ½ teaspoon black pepper
- ½ pound boneless skinless chicken thighs, cut into ¾-inch pieces
- 1 can (about 14 ounces) stewed tomatoes, undrained
- 1 can (about 14 ounces) chicken broth
- 1 can (about 15 ounces) cannellini beans, rinsed and drained
- Hot pepper sauce (optional)

1. Cut off, chop and reserve ¼ cup feathery fennel tops. Chop bulb into ½-inch pieces. Heat oil in large saucepan over medium heat. Add chopped fennel bulb; cook 5 minutes, stirring occasionally.

2. Sprinkle rosemary and pepper over chicken; add to saucepan. Cook and stir 2 minutes. Add tomatoes and broth; bring to a boil. Cover; simmer 10 minutes. Stir in beans; simmer, uncovered, 15 minutes or until chicken is cooked through and sauce thickens.

3. Season to taste with hot pepper sauce, if desired. Ladle into 4 shallow bowls; garnish with reserved fennel tops.

Makes 4 servings

Prep Time: 15 minutes
Cook Time: 35 minutes

BREAD BOWL CHICKEN STEW

- 2 medium Yukon Gold potatoes, peeled and chopped (about 1½ cups)
- 1 cup chopped carrots
- ¾ teaspoon salt, divided
- 4 (5-inch) round sourdough or Italian bread loaves
- Nonstick cooking spray
- 2 tablespoons butter
- 12 ounces boneless skinless chicken breasts, cut into bite-size pieces
- 2 tablespoons all-purpose flour
- ¼ teaspoon black pepper
- ⅛ teaspoon dried thyme
- ⅛ teaspoon paprika
- 1 cup chicken broth
- 1 cup frozen peas, thawed
- 1 green onion, minced

1. Preheat oven to 400°F. Place potatoes, carrots and ½ teaspoon salt in medium saucepan; add water to cover. Bring to a boil over high heat. Reduce heat to medium; cook 15 minutes or until vegetables are tender. Drain and set aside.

2. Cut off top third of each bread loaf. Pull out soft insides; reserve for another use. Spray inside of loaves with cooking spray. Place bread on baking sheet. Bake 10 minutes; set aside.

3. Melt butter in large saucepan over medium heat. Add chicken; brown 5 minutes, stirring occasionally. Add flour, remaining ¼ teaspoon salt, pepper, thyme and paprika. Cook and stir 1 to 2 minutes. Gradually add broth; cook and stir until mixture thickens. Add potatoes and carrots. Add peas and green onion. Simmer 5 minutes. Spoon stew into bread bowls.

Makes 4 servings

CHICKEN & BARLEY STEW

- 1 cup thinly sliced celery
- 1 medium onion, coarsely chopped
- 1 carrot, thinly sliced
- ½ cup medium pearled barley
- 1 clove garlic, minced
- 1 whole chicken (about 3 pounds), cut up
- 1 tablespoon olive oil
- 2½ cups chicken broth
- 1 can (about 14 ounces) diced tomatoes
- ¾ teaspoon salt
- ½ teaspoon dried basil
- ¼ teaspoon black pepper

Slow Cooker Directions

1. Place celery, onion, carrot, barley and garlic in slow cooker.

2. Remove and discard skin from chicken pieces. Separate drumsticks from thighs. Trim off and discard back bone from breasts. Save wings for another use. Heat oil in large skillet over medium-high heat; brown chicken pieces on all sides. Place chicken in slow cooker.

3. Add broth, tomatoes, salt, basil and pepper to slow cooker. Cook on LOW 7 to 8 hours or HIGH 4 hours or until barley is tender. Remove chicken from slow cooker; let cool slightly. Remove and discard bones. Cut chicken into bite-size pieces, stir into soup.

Makes 4 servings

TIP Pearled barley has been polished many times to remove the bran and most of the germ. It has a nutty flavor and slightly chewy texture and is high in fiber, making it a tasty, nutritious option.

APPLE AND CHICKEN SOUP

- **1 sweet potato (8 ounces)**
- **1 tablespoon olive oil**
- **2 stalks celery, thinly sliced**
- **½ medium onion, chopped**
- **1 teaspoon dried thyme**
- **½ teaspoon dried rosemary**
- **¼ teaspoon dried sage**
- **¼ teaspoon ground nutmeg**
- **2 cans (about 14 ounces each) chicken broth**
- **1 cup apple juice**
- **1 large McIntosh apple, peeled and chopped**
- **⅔ cup uncooked small pasta shells**
- **¾ pound boneless skinless chicken breasts**

1. Pierce sweet potato in several places with fork. Microwave on HIGH 6 to 8 minutes or until almost tender; set aside. (Sweet potato will finish cooking and become tender as it stands.)

2. Heat oil in large saucepan over medium-high heat. Add celery, onion, thyme, rosemary, sage and nutmeg. Cover and cook 3 to 4 minutes or until onion is tender. Add broth, juice and apple. Bring to a boil over high heat; stir in pasta. Reduce heat to medium-high; boil, uncovered, 8 to 10 minutes.

3. Cut chicken into ¼-inch-wide strips. Peel skin from sweet potato; cut into 1-inch pieces. Add chicken and sweet potato to soup. Reduce heat to medium; simmer 3 to 5 minutes or until chicken is cooked through and pasta is tender.

Makes 4 to 6 servings

Serving Suggestion: Serve with warm herb-cheese bread.

Prep and Cook Time: 25 minutes

CHUNKY CHICKEN PICADILLO CHILI

- 2 teaspoons *each* ground cumin and chili powder
- 1 teaspoon salt
- 1/4 teaspoon ground cinnamon
- 1 pound boneless, skinless chicken breasts, cut into 1-inch chunks
- 1 tablespoon vegetable oil
- 1 large onion, chopped
- 4 cloves garlic, minced
- 2 cans (14 1/2 ounces each) Mexican style diced tomatoes, undrained
- 1/2 cup chipotle salsa or medium heat salsa
- 3/4 cup SUN•MAID® Raisins
- 1 can (16 ounces) red or black beans, drained

Optional toppings:
Chopped cilantro, shredded cheddar cheese, sour cream

COMBINE cumin, chili powder, salt, and cinnamon. Coat chicken evenly with seasonings.

HEAT oil in a large saucepan over medium heat.

ADD onion and cook 5 minutes, stirring occasionally.

ADD chicken and garlic. Cook 3 minutes, stirring occasionally.

STIR in tomatoes, salsa and raisins. Bring to simmer.

COVER and simmer 10 minutes

STIR in beans. Cover and continue to simmer 5 minutes. Ladle into bowls and serve with desired toppings.

Makes 6 servings

Prep Time: about 10 minutes
Cook Time: 20 minutes

CARIBBEAN CALLALOO SOUP

- 1 butternut squash (about 1½ pounds)
- ¾ pound boneless skinless chicken breasts
- 1 teaspoon olive oil
- 1 large onion, chopped
- 4 cloves garlic, minced
- 3 cans (about 14 ounces each) chicken broth
- 2 jalapeño peppers,* seeded and minced
- 2 teaspoons dried thyme
- ½ (10-ounce) package spinach, stemmed and torn
- ¼ cup plus 2 tablespoons shredded coconut

**Jalapeño peppers can sting and irritate the skin, so wear rubber gloves when handling peppers and do not touch your eyes.*

1. Peel squash; cut in half lengthwise and discard seeds. Cut into ½-inch cubes. Slice chicken crosswise into very thin strips.

2. Heat oil in large nonstick skillet over medium-low heat. Add onion and garlic; cover and cook 5 minutes or until onion is tender, stirring frequently.

3. Add squash, broth, jalapeño peppers and thyme; bring to a boil over high heat. Reduce heat to low; simmer, covered, 15 to 20 minutes or until squash is very tender.

4. Add chicken; cover and cook 2 minutes or until chicken is cooked through. Remove skillet from heat; stir in spinach until wilted. Ladle into bowls and sprinkle with coconut. *Makes 6 servings*

CHICKEN AND CHILE PEPPER STEW

1 pound boneless skinless chicken thighs, cut into ½-inch pieces
1 pound small potatoes, sliced
1 cup chopped onion
2 poblano peppers, seeded and cut into bite-size pieces
3 cloves garlic, minced
1 jalapeño pepper,* seeded and finely chopped
3 cups chicken broth
1 can (about 14 ounces) diced tomatoes
2 tablespoons chili powder
1 teaspoon dried oregano

**Jalapeño peppers can sting and irritate the skin, so wear rubber gloves when handling peppers and do not touch your eyes.*

Slow Cooker Directions

Combine chicken, potatoes, onion, poblano peppers, garlic and jalapeño pepper in 5-quart slow cooker. Stir together broth, tomatoes, chili powder and oregano in large bowl. Pour broth mixture over chicken mixture; mix well. Cover; cook on LOW 8 to 9 hours. *Makes 6 servings*

FRENCH COUNTRY CHICKEN STEW

¼ pound sliced bacon, diced
4 boneless, skinless chicken breast halves, cut into 1-inch pieces
1 medium onion, chopped
2 cloves garlic, minced
1 teaspoon dried thyme leaves, crushed
1 can (14½ ounces) DEL MONTE® Cut Green Beans, drained
1 can (15 ounces) kidney beans, drained
1 can (14½ ounces) DEL MONTE® Stewed Tomatoes - Original Recipe
Salt and pepper to taste

1. Cook and stir bacon in large skillet over medium-high heat until almost crisp. Add chicken, onion, garlic and thyme.

2. Cook and stir until onion and garlic are soft, about 5 minutes. Pour off drippings.

3. Add remaining ingredients; bring to a boil over high heat. Reduce heat to low. Simmer, uncovered, 10 minutes. *Makes 4 servings*

• CHICKEN AND CHILE PEPPER STEW •

SOUTHWESTERN CHICKEN SOUP

- ½ teaspoon salt
- ¼ teaspoon garlic powder
- ¼ teaspoon black pepper
- 1 pound boneless skinless chicken breasts, cut into bite-size pieces
- 1 tablespoon olive oil
- 1 medium onion, halved and sliced
- 1 jalapeño pepper,* seeded and chopped (optional)
- 4 cans (about 14 ounces each) chicken broth
- 2 cups diced peeled potatoes
- 2 small zucchini, sliced
- 1½ cups frozen corn
- 1 cup diced tomato
- 2 tablespoons fresh lime or lemon juice
- 1 tablespoon chopped fresh cilantro

**Jalapeño peppers can sting and irritate the skin, so wear rubber gloves when handling peppers and do not touch your eyes.*

1. Combine salt, garlic powder and black pepper in small bowl; sprinkle evenly over chicken.

2. Heat oil in Dutch oven over medium-high heat. Add chicken; cook 4 minutes or until brown on all sides. Add onion and jalapeño pepper, if desired; cook 2 minutes or until tender, adding a little broth if needed to prevent burning.

3. Add broth; bring to a boil over high heat. Stir in potatoes. Reduce heat; simmer 5 minutes. Add zucchini, corn and tomato; cook 10 minutes or until vegetables are tender. Stir in lime juice and cilantro just before serving.

Makes 6 servings

Prep Time: 10 minutes
Cook Time: 22 minutes

CHICKEN & WHITE BEAN STEW

1 tablespoon olive oil
2 medium carrots, sliced (about 2 cups)
1 medium onion, thinly sliced
2 cloves garlic, finely chopped
1 tablespoon balsamic vinegar
1 pound boneless, skinless chicken breast halves or thighs, cut into chunks
1 jar (1 pound 10 ounces) RAGÚ® Old World Style® Pasta Sauce
2 cans (15 ounces each) cannellini or white kidney beans, rinsed and drained
Pinch crushed red pepper flakes (optional)

1. In 12-inch skillet, heat olive oil over medium heat and cook carrots, onion and garlic, stirring occasionally, 5 minutes or until vegetables are tender. Stir in vinegar and cook 1 minute. Remove vegetables; set aside.

2. In same skillet, thoroughly brown chicken over medium-high heat. Return vegetables to skillet. Stir in Pasta Sauce, beans and red pepper flakes. Bring to a boil over high heat. Reduce heat to medium and simmer, covered, stirring occasionally, 15 minutes or until chicken is thoroughly cooked. Garnish, if desired, with fresh parsley and serve with toasted Italian bread. *Makes 6 servings*

SUN–DRIED TOMATO WRAPS WITH FRIED CHICKEN

½ cup ranch dressing
4 large sun-dried tomato flour tortillas, warmed
3 cups shredded lettuce
4 ounces sliced Monterey Jack cheese
1 can (2½ ounces) sliced black olives, drained
4 to 8 fried chicken tenders (about 1 pound), cut in half lengthwise
Hot pepper sauce (optional)

1. Spoon 2 tablespoons dressing down center of each tortilla. Top with equal amounts lettuce, cheese, olives and chicken. Sprinkle with pepper sauce, if desired.

2. Roll up jelly-roll style. Serve immediately. *Makes 4 servings*

Tip: If fried chicken tenders are not available in your supermarket deli, substitute thawed frozen chicken fingers.

APRICOT CHICKEN SANDWICHES

6 ounces diced cooked chicken
2 tablespoons chopped pitted fresh apricot
2 tablespoons apricot fruit spread
4 slices whole wheat bread
4 lettuce leaves

1. Combine chicken, apricot and fruit spread in medium bowl.

2. Top 2 bread slices with lettuce. Top evenly with chicken mixture and top with remaining 2 bread slices. Cut sandwiches into quarters.

Makes 4 servings

CHICKEN & SPINACH MUFFULETTA

6 boneless skinless chicken breasts
Salt and black pepper
1 tablespoon olive oil
¼ cup prepared pesto
¼ cup chopped pitted black olives
¼ cup chopped pitted green olives
1 round loaf (16 ounces) Hawaiian or French bread
2 cups torn stemmed spinach
4 slices mozzarella cheese

1. Season chicken with salt and pepper. Heat oil in large skillet over medium heat. Add chicken; cook 8 minutes or until no longer pink in center, turning once. Cut chicken into strips.

2. Combine pesto and olives in small bowl. Cut bread in half horizontally. Spread bottom half of bread with pesto mixture. Top with spinach, chicken, cheese and top half of bread. Cut into wedges.

Makes 6 servings

Cook's Note: Muffuletta sandwiches can be served warm or cold. To heat, simply wrap the whole sandwich in foil. Bake in preheated 375°F oven for 15 minutes or until the cheese begins to melt.

• APRICOT CHICKEN SANDWICH •

BLACKENED CHICKEN SALAD PITAS

- 1 tablespoon paprika
- 1 teaspoon onion powder
- ½ teaspoon garlic powder
- ½ teaspoon dried oregano
- ½ teaspoon dried thyme
- ¼ teaspoon salt
- ¼ teaspoon white pepper
- ¼ teaspoon ground red pepper
- ¼ teaspoon black pepper
- 1 pound boneless skinless chicken breasts
- 4 pita bread rounds
- 1 cup baby spinach
- 2 small tomatoes, cut into 8 slices
- 8 thin slices cucumber
- ½ cup ranch dressing

1. Prepare grill for direct cooking. Combine paprika, onion powder, garlic powder, oregano, thyme, salt, white pepper, red pepper and black pepper in small bowl; rub all over chicken.

2. Grill chicken, covered, over medium-high heat 10 to 15 minutes or until no longer pink in center, turning once. Cool slightly; cut into thin strips.

3. Wrap 2 pitas in paper towels. Microwave on HIGH 20 to 30 seconds or just until warm. Repeat with remaining pitas. Cut in half horizontally.

4. Divide chicken, spinach, tomatoes, cucumber and ranch dressing among pita bread halves. Serve warm.

Makes 4 servings

• BLACKENED CHICKEN SALAD PITA •

CHICKEN AND MOZZARELLA MELTS

- 2 cloves garlic, crushed
- 4 boneless skinless chicken breasts (about 1 pound)
- Salt and black pepper
- Nonstick cooking spray
- 1 tablespoon prepared pesto
- 4 hard rolls, split
- 12 baby spinach leaves
- 8 fresh basil leaves*
- 3 plum tomatoes, sliced
- ½ cup (2 ounces) shredded mozzarella cheese

**Omit basil leaves if fresh are unavailable. Do not substitute dried basil.*

1. Preheat oven to 350°F. Rub garlic on all surfaces of chicken; season with salt and pepper. Spray medium nonstick skillet with cooking spray; heat over medium heat. Add chicken; cook 10 to 15 minutes or until no longer pink in center, turning once.

2. Brush pesto on rolls; layer with spinach, basil and tomatoes. Top with chicken; sprinkle with cheese. Wrap sandwiches in foil; bake 10 minutes or until cheese is melted. *Makes 4 servings*

ASIAN WRAPS

- Nonstick cooking spray
- 8 ounces boneless skinless chicken breasts or thighs, cut into ½-inch pieces
- 1 teaspoon minced fresh ginger
- 1 teaspoon minced garlic
- ¼ teaspoon red pepper flakes
- 4 cups (about 8 ounces) coleslaw mix
- ½ cup sliced green onions
- ¼ cup teriyaki sauce
- 4 (10-inch) flour tortillas
- 8 teaspoons plum fruit spread

1. Spray nonstick large deep skillet or wok with cooking spray; heat over medium-high heat. Stir-fry chicken 2 minutes. Add ginger, garlic and pepper flakes; stir-fry 2 minutes. Add coleslaw mix, green onions and teriyaki sauce; stir-fry 4 minutes or until chicken is cooked through.

2. Spread each tortilla with 2 teaspoons fruit spread; evenly spoon chicken mixture down center of tortillas. Roll up to form wraps. *Makes 4 servings*

MEDITERRANEAN GRILLED CHICKEN BLT

- 4 chicken breast halves, skinless and boneless, 1 pound
- 4 sun-dried tomatoes, packed in oil
- 8 fresh oregano sprigs
- 2 tablespoons oil from the sun-dried tomatoes
- Salt and freshly ground black pepper to taste

Tomato Mayonnaise

- ¼ cup mayonnaise
- 2 teaspoons tomato paste
- 1 teaspoon fresh oregano, chopped
- ½ freshly ground black pepper

The Fixin's

- 8 slices bacon, cooked
- 4 romaine lettuce leaves
- 2 large, very ripe tomatoes, sliced
- 4 pieces focaccia, 4 to 6 inches square, cut in half horizontally

Prepare the coals for the grill or preheat the broiler.

Use a thin, sharp knife to slice a pocket in the side of each chicken breast. Into each pocket, slip a sun-dried tomato and 2 sprigs of oregano. Rub the chicken with 1 tablespoon oil from the sun-dried tomatoes and season with salt and pepper. Baste with other tablespoon oil from tomatoes while grilling.

Grill the chicken until the outside is nicely charred and the internal temperature is 180°F. when tested with a thermometer. The chicken should feel firm to the touch.

While the chicken is cooking, stir the ingredients for the Tomato Mayonnaise together in a small bowl.

Remove chicken to cutting board and cut diagonally into long, thin slices.

To assemble the sandwiches, spread the focaccia (both tops and bottoms) with the Tomato Mayonnaise. Arrange chicken slices on the bottom piece of focaccia. Top each sandwich with 2 slices bacon, tomato slices and lettuce leaf. Set the top of the bread in place and cut the sandwich in half to serve.

Makes 4 servings

Favorite recipe from **National Chicken Council**

ITALIAN CHICKEN PANINI

6 small portobello mushroom caps
½ cup plus 2 tablespoons balsamic vinaigrette dressing
1 loaf (16 ounces) Italian bread, cut into 12 slices
12 slices provolone cheese
1½ cups chopped cooked chicken
1 jar (12 ounces) roasted red peppers, drained

1. Brush mushrooms with 2 tablespoons dressing. Cook mushrooms in medium skillet over medium-high heat 5 to 7 minutes or until soft; cut diagonally into ½-inch slices.

2. Layer 6 bread slices with cheese slice, chicken, mushrooms, roasted red peppers and another cheese slice. Top with remaining bread slices. Brush outsides of sandwiches with remaining dressing.

3. Preheat grill pan and panini press over medium heat 5 minutes. Grill sandwiches 4 to 6 minutes or until cheese is melted and bread is golden, turning once. *Makes 6 sandwiches*

Cook's Note: A rotisserie chicken will yield just enough chopped chicken for this recipe.

TIP If you don't have a grill pan and panini press, grill sandwiches in a nonstick skillet. Place a clean heavy pan on top of sandwiches to weigh them down while cooking.

CHICKEN PATTIES WITH LEMON–MUSTARD SAUCE

- Lemon-Mustard Sauce (recipe follows)
- 1 pound ground chicken
- ¼ cup finely chopped onion
- ¼ cup finely chopped red or green bell pepper
- 1 clove garlic, minced
- 2 tablespoons plain dry bread crumbs
- ¼ teaspoon salt
- ¼ teaspoon black pepper
- Nonstick cooking spray
- 4 pita bread rounds, toasted

1. Prepare Lemon-Mustard Sauce.

2. Combine chicken, onion, bell pepper, garlic, bread crumbs, salt and black pepper in medium bowl; shape into 4 patties.

3. Spray large nonstick skillet with cooking spray; heat over medium heat. Add patties; cook 8 minutes or until cooked through (165°F), turning once.

4. Cut pitas in half horizontally. Fill pitas with lettuce, patties and sauce.

Makes 4 servings

Prep Time: 10 minutes
Cook Time: 10 minutes

LEMON–MUSTARD SAUCE

- ½ cup plain yogurt
- 2 tablespoons sour cream
- 2 tablespoons Dijon mustard
- 1 clove garlic, minced
- ½ teaspoon grated lemon peel

Combine all ingredients in small bowl; mix well.

Makes about ¾ cup

GRAB & GO BARBECUE CHICKEN SANDWICHES

- 1 tablespoon olive or vegetable oil
- 2 pounds skinless, boneless chicken thighs (about 16)
- 1 large red pepper, cut into 2-inch-long strips (about 1½ cups)
- 1 large sweet onion, thinly sliced (about 1 cup)
- 1 can (10¾ ounces) CAMPBELL'S® Condensed Tomato Soup
- ¾ cup water
- ¼ cup cider vinegar
- 2 tablespoons packed brown sugar
- 1 teaspoon ground chipotle chili pepper
- 1 bag (13 ounces) PEPPERIDGE FARM® Sandwich Buns
- Shredded Cheddar cheese (optional)

1. Heat the oil in a 5-quart saucepot over medium-high heat. Add the chicken in 2 batches and cook for 10 minutes until it's well browned on both sides. Remove the chicken and set aside.

2. Add the pepper and onion and cook until the vegetables are tender-crisp.

3. Stir the soup, water, vinegar, brown sugar and chili pepper into the saucepot. Heat to a boil. Return the chicken to the saucepot and reduce the heat to low. Cover and cook for 20 minutes.

4. Remove the chicken from the sauce, but continue to cook the sauce. Using two forks or your fingers, pull the cooked chicken into shreds and tear into bite-size pieces. Return the chicken to the saucepot.

5. Cook for 10 minutes more or until the mixture thickens.

6. Divide the chicken mixture among the buns. Top with cheese, if desired.

Makes 8 servings

Prep Time: 10 minutes
Cook Time: 45 minutes

FIESTA CHICKEN SANDWICH

- 1 tablespoon plus 2 teaspoons olive oil, divided
- ½ small onion, sliced
- ½ medium red bell pepper, sliced
- 6 ounces chicken tenders, cut in half lengthwise and crosswise
- ½ cup guacamole
- 6 slices (1 ounce each) pepper jack cheese
- 1 package (10 ounces) 8-inch mini pizza crusts

1. Heat 1 tablespoon oil in large nonstick skillet over medium-high heat. Add onion and bell pepper; cook and stir 3 minutes or until crisp-tender. Remove vegetables with slotted spoon; set aside. Add chicken to skillet; cook and stir 4 minutes or until cooked through. Cool slightly.

2. Layer guacamole, chicken, vegetables and cheese evenly on 1 pizza crust; top with remaining pizza crust. Brush sandwich lightly with remaining 2 teaspoons oil.

3. Wipe out skillet with paper towel; heat over medium heat. Add sandwich; cook 4 minutes per side or until cheese melts and sandwich is golden brown. Cut into wedges. *Makes 2 servings*

REUBEN CHICKEN MELTS

- 4 boneless skinless chicken breasts
- 1 large onion, cut into ½-inch slices
- 1¼ cups Thousand Island dressing, divided
- 1½ cups (6 ounces) shredded Swiss cheese
- 4 French rolls, split
- 2 cups shredded red cabbage

1. Preheat grill for direct cooking. Brush chicken and onion with ½ cup dressing. Grill chicken 12 minutes or until no longer pink in center, turning once. Sprinkle chicken evenly with cheese during last minute of cooking. Grill onions 8 minutes or until browned and tender. Toast rolls.

2. Combine ¼ cup salad dressing and cabbage; mix well.

3. Spread rolls with remaining ½ cup salad dressing. Place chicken on roll bottoms. Top with onion, cabbage mixture and roll tops. Serve immediately. *Makes 4 servings*

GRILLED CUBAN PARTY SANDWICH

- ¾ cup plus 2 tablespoons olive oil, divided
- 6 tablespoons fresh lime juice
- 4 cloves garlic, minced
- Salt and black pepper
- 2 boneless skinless chicken breasts
- 1 yellow onion, cut into ½-inch slices
- 1 loaf ciabatta bread (1 pound), cut in half lengthwise
- ¼ cup chopped fresh cilantro
- 6 ounces fresh mozzarella, sliced
- 1 medium tomato, thinly sliced

1. For marinade, combine ¾ cup oil, lime juice and garlic in medium bowl; mix well. Season with salt and pepper.

2. Pour ¼ cup of marinade into resealable food storage bag. Add chicken; seal bag and turn to coat. Refrigerate up to 2 hours. Refrigerate remaining marinade.

3. Brush grid with 1 tablespoon oil. Prepare grill for direct cooking. Thread onion onto skewers; brush with remaining 1 tablespoon oil and season with salt and pepper. Drain chicken; discard marinade. Grill chicken 12 to 15 minutes or until no longer pink in center, turning once. Grill onion 8 to 12 minutes or until soft and browned, turning once. Meanwhile, toast cut sides of bread.

4. Let chicken stand 10 minutes; cut into thin slices. Remove onion from skewers and separate into rings.

5. Brush reserved marinade onto cut sides of bread. Sprinkle with cilantro. Layer bottom of bread with cheese, tomato, chicken and onion; add top of bread. Press down firmly to compact sandwich; wrap with foil. Place on grid over direct heat. Top with large heavy skillet or brick wrapped in foil to flatten. Grill 4 to 6 minutes or until cheese melts. Cut into 6 pieces; serve immediately. *Makes 6 servings*

RANCH CHICKEN SALAD PITAS

- 4 cups torn mixed spring greens
- 2 cups chopped cooked chicken
- ½ cup chopped green bell pepper or poblano pepper
- ½ cup ranch dressing
- 4 whole wheat pita bread rounds, halved
- Black pepper (optional)

1. Toss greens, chicken, bell pepper and dressing in large bowl. Microwave pita on HIGH 12 to 15 seconds.

2. Fill pita halves with salad mixture. Sprinkle with black pepper, if desired. *Makes 4 servings*

SHREDDED BBQ CHICKEN SANDWICHES

- 1 jar (1 pound 10 ounces) RAGÚ® Old World Style® Pasta Sauce
- 3 tablespoons firmly packed brown sugar
- 2 tablespoons apple cider vinegar
- 1½ tablespoons chili powder
- 2 teaspoons garlic powder
- 1½ teaspoons onion powder
- 4 boneless, skinless chicken breast halves (about 1¼ pounds)
- 6 hamburger buns or round rolls

1. In 6-quart saucepot, cook Pasta Sauce, brown sugar, vinegar, chili powder, garlic powder and onion powder over medium heat, stirring occasionally, 5 minutes.

2. Season chicken, if desired, with salt and ground black pepper. Add chicken to sauce. Reduce heat to medium-low and simmer, covered, stirring occasionally, 20 minutes or until chicken is no longer pink in center. Remove saucepot from heat.

3. Remove chicken from sauce. Using two forks, shred chicken. Return shredded chicken to sauce and heat through. To serve, arrange chicken mixture on buns and garnish, if desired, with shredded Cheddar cheese. *Makes 6 servings*

Prep Time: 5 minutes
Cook Time: 30 minutes

• RANCH CHICKEN SALAD PITA •

CHICKEN ENCHILADA ROLL–UPS

- ½ cup plus 2 tablespoons all-purpose flour, divided
- ½ teaspoon salt
- 1½ pounds chicken tenders
- 2 tablespoons butter
- 1 cup chicken broth
- 1 small onion, diced
- ¼ to ½ cup sliced jalapeño peppers*
- ½ teaspoon dried oregano
- 2 tablespoons whipping cream or milk
- 6 (7- to 8-inch) flour tortillas
- 6 thin slices American cheese or American cheese with jalapeño peppers

**Jalapeño peppers can sting and irritate the skin, so wear rubber gloves when handling peppers and do not touch your eyes.*

Slow Cooker Directions

1. Combine ½ cup flour and salt in resealable food storage bag. Add chicken and shake to coat with flour mixture. Melt butter in large skillet over medium heat. Brown chicken in batches, turning once. Place chicken in slow cooker.

2. Add broth to skillet and scrape up any browned bits. Pour broth mixture into slow cooker. Add onion, jalapeño peppers and oregano. Cover; cook on LOW 7 to 8 hours or on HIGH 3 to 4 hours.

3. Blend remaining 2 tablespoons flour and cream in small bowl until smooth. Stir into chicken mixture. Cook, uncovered, on HIGH 15 minutes or until thickened. Spoon chicken mixture onto center of tortillas. Top with 1 cheese slice. Roll up tortillas and serve.

Makes 6 servings

Serving Suggestion: This rich, creamy chicken mixture can also be served over hot cooked rice.

Prep Time: 20 minutes
Cook Time: about 7 to 8 hours (LOW) or about 3 to 4 hours (HIGH)

• CHICKEN ENCHILADA ROLL–UP •

JAMAICAN CHICKEN SANDWICH

- 1 teaspoon Jerk Seasoning (recipe follows)
- 4 boneless skinless chicken breasts
- 2 tablespoons mayonnaise
- 2 tablespoons plain yogurt
- 1 tablespoon mango chutney
- 4 onion rolls, split and toasted
- 4 lettuce leaves
- 12 slices peeled mango or papaya

1. Prepare Jerk Seasoning. Sprinkle chicken with 1 teaspoon seasoning; set aside. Combine mayonnaise, yogurt and chutney in small bowl; set aside.

2. Spray grid with nonstick cooking spray. Prepare grill for direct cooking. Grill chicken 10 to 15 minutes or until no longer pink in center, turning once.

3. Spread 1 tablespoonful mayonnaise mixture onto cut sides of rolls. Place chicken on bottoms of rolls; top with lettuce, mango slices and tops of rolls.

Makes 4 servings

JERK SEASONING

- 1½ teaspoons salt
- 1½ teaspoons ground allspice
- 1 teaspoon sugar
- 1 teaspoon ground thyme
- 1 teaspoon black pepper
- ½ teaspoon garlic powder
- ½ teaspoon ground red pepper
- ¼ teaspoon ground cinnamon
- ¼ teaspoon ground nutmeg

Combine all ingredients in small bowl. Store any leftover Jerk Seasoning in airtight container in a cool dry place.

Makes about 2 tablespoons

EASY THAI CHICKEN SANDWICHES

- ¼ cup peanut butter
- 2 tablespoons honey
- 2 tablespoons soy sauce
- ½ teaspoon garlic powder
- ½ teaspoon ground ginger
- 4 boneless skinless chicken breasts
- 4 onion or kaiser rolls, split
- Lettuce leaves
- 1 cup sliced cucumbers
- 1 cup bean sprouts
- ¼ cup sliced green onions

1. Preheat oven to 400°F. Line baking pan with foil. Combine peanut butter, honey, soy sauce, garlic powder and ginger in small bowl; stir until well blended. Reserve ¼ cup peanut butter mixture.

2. Place chicken on prepared baking pan. Spread remaining peanut butter mixture over chicken. Bake 20 minutes or until chicken is no longer pink in center.

3. Spread reserved peanut butter mixture on rolls. Top with lettuce, cucumbers, bean sprouts and chicken; sprinkle with green onions. *Makes 4 servings*

CHICKEN, FETA AND PEPPER SUBS

- 1 pound boneless, skinless chicken breasts
- 3 tablespoons olive oil, divided
- 2 teaspoons Original TABASCO® brand Pepper Sauce
- ½ teaspoon salt
- ½ teaspoon ground cumin
- 1 red bell pepper, cut into strips
- 1 yellow or green bell pepper, cut into strips
- ½ cup crumbled feta cheese
- 4 (6-inch) French rolls

Cut chicken breasts into thin strips. Heat 1 tablespoon oil in 12-inch skillet over medium-high heat. Add chicken; cook until well browned on all sides, stirring frequently. Stir in TABASCO® Sauce, salt and cumin. Remove mixture to medium bowl. Add remaining 2 tablespoons oil to same skillet over medium heat. Add bell peppers; cook about 5 minutes or until tender-crisp, stirring occasionally. Toss with chicken and feta cheese. To serve, cut rolls crosswise in half. Cover bottom halves with chicken mixture and top with remaining roll halves. *Makes 4 servings*

CHICKEN BURGERS WITH WHITE CHEDDAR

1¼ pounds ground chicken
1 cup plain dry bread crumbs
½ cup diced red bell pepper
½ cup ground walnuts
¼ cup sliced green onions
¼ cup beer
2 tablespoons chopped fresh parsley
2 tablespoons fresh lemon juice
2 cloves garlic, minced
¾ teaspoon salt
⅛ teaspoon black pepper
Nonstick cooking spray
4 slices white Cheddar cheese
4 whole wheat buns
Lettuce leaves

Combine chicken, bread crumbs, bell pepper, walnuts, green onions, beer, parsley, lemon juice, garlic, salt and black pepper in large bowl; mix lightly. Shape chicken mixture into 4 patties. Spray large skillet with cooking spray; heat over medium-high heat. Cook patties 12 to 14 minutes or until cooked through, turning once. Place cheese on patties; cover and cook just until cheese is melted. Serve patties on buns with lettuce. *Makes 4 servings*

TROPICAL CHICKEN SALAD POCKETS

3 cups diced cooked chicken
1 can (20 ounces) pineapple chunks in juice, drained, juice reserved
3 green onions, thinly sliced
2 tablespoons chopped fresh cilantro
Tropical Dressing (recipe follows)
4 pocket breads, split
Lettuce leaves

In bowl, place chicken, pineapple, green onions, and cilantro. Pour dressing over chicken mixture and toss to mix. Line each pocket bread with lettuce leaf; fill with chicken salad. *Makes 4 servings*

Tropical Dressing: In small bowl, mix together ½ cup reduced-fat mayonnaise, 1 tablespoon lime juice, 1 tablespoon reserved pineapple juice, 1 teaspoon sugar, 1 teaspoon curry powder, ½ teaspoon salt, and ¼ teaspoon grated lime peel. Makes about ⅔ cup dressing.

Favorite recipe from **Delmarva Poultry Industry, Inc.**

• CHICKEN BURGER WITH WHITE CHEDDAR •

HOT CHICKEN BAGUETTES

1 red bell pepper, cut into chunks
1 to 2 carrots, sliced
½ cup sliced celery
1 small onion, chopped
1 clove garlic, minced
¼ teaspoon dried oregano
¼ teaspoon red pepper flakes
¼ cup all-purpose flour
1 teaspoon salt
½ teaspoon black pepper
6 boneless skinless chicken breasts
1 tablespoon vegetable oil
1 can (about 14 ounces) chicken broth
6 small French bread baguettes, split and toasted
6 slices Swiss cheese (optional)

Slow Cooker Directions

1. Place bell pepper, carrots, celery, onion, garlic, oregano and pepper flakes in slow cooker.

2. Combine flour, salt and black pepper in resealable food storage bag. Add chicken, 2 pieces at a time; shake to coat with flour mixture. Heat oil in large skillet over medium-high heat. Add chicken; brown 4 to 6 minutes, turning once.

3. Place chicken in slow cooker; add broth. Cover; cook on LOW 5 to 6 hours.

4. Place 1 chicken breast on each baguette; top with vegetables. Spoon 1 to 2 tablespoons broth mixture over vegetables and top with 1 slice cheese, if desired. *Makes 6 servings*

Prep Time: 15 minutes
Cook Time: 5 to 6 hours

MEXICAN PITA PILE–UPS

- 1 cup shredded cooked chicken
- ¼ cup canned chopped mild green chiles
- 1 tablespoon fresh lime juice
- 1 teaspoon ground cumin
- 2 whole wheat pita bread rounds
- 1 cup chopped seeded tomato
- ¼ cup chopped fresh cilantro (optional)
- 1 can (2¼ ounces) sliced black olives, drained
- ¾ cup (3 ounces) shredded sharp Cheddar cheese

Microwave Directions

Combine chicken, chiles, lime juice and cumin in medium bowl. Place pitas on microwavable plates; top evenly with chicken mixture, tomato, cilantro, if desired, olives and cheese. Microwave each topped pita on HIGH 1 minute or until cheese is melted. Let stand 2 to 3 minutes before serving. *Makes 2 servings*

CHINESE CHICKEN SALAD SANDWICHES

- ¼ cup soy sauce
- ¼ cup rice wine vinegar
- ¼ cup vegetable or peanut oil
- ¼ cup roasted sesame seed oil
- 2 tablespoons fresh ginger, minced
- 4 teaspoons sugar
- 4 teaspoons dry mustard
- 2 pounds chicken breast, boned, skinned, steamed and cubed
- 1 large red onion (about 9 to 11 ounces), cut into narrow wedges
- 1 cup pea pods, fresh or thawed frozen, slivered
- 6 crusty round rolls, split, buttered
- Lettuce or watercress
- 4 teaspoons sesame seeds, toasted
- Crispy noodles (optional)

Mix dressing of soy sauce, vinegar, oils, ginger, sugar and mustard. Add chicken, onions and pea pods. Toss well. Chill at least 4 hours to blend flavors. Fill each roll with lettuce and chicken salad. Sprinkle with sesame seeds. Serve with crispy noodles, if desired. *Makes 6 servings*

Favorite recipe from **National Onion Association**

• MEXICAN PITA PILE–UP •

TOASTED COBB SALAD SANDWICHES

- ½ ripe avocado
- 1 green onion, chopped
- ½ teaspoon fresh lemon juice
- Salt and black pepper
- 2 kaiser rolls, split
- 4 ounces thinly sliced deli chicken or turkey
- 4 slices crisp-cooked bacon
- 1 hard-cooked egg, sliced
- 2 slices (1 ounce each) Cheddar cheese
- 2 ounces crumbled blue cheese
- Tomato slices (optional)
- Olive oil

1. Mash avocado in small bowl; stir in green onion and lemon juice. Season with salt and pepper. Spread avocado mixture on cut sides of roll tops. Layer bottoms of rolls with chicken, bacon, egg, cheeses and tomato, if desired. Close sandwiches with roll tops. Brush outsides of sandwiches lightly with oil.

2. Heat large nonstick skillet over medium heat. Add sandwiches; cook 8 to 10 minutes or until cheese is melted and sandwiches are golden brown, turning once.

Makes 2 sandwiches

WARM BACON AND CHICKEN SALAD SANDWICHES

- 1 (10-ounce) can HORMEL® chunk breast of chicken, drained and flaked
- ½ cup mayonnaise or salad dressing
- ⅓ cup diced celery
- ¼ cup minced onion
- ½ teaspoon lemon juice
- ½ teaspoon Worcestershire sauce
- ⅛ teaspoon ground black pepper
- Leaf lettuce
- 4 slices whole wheat bread, toasted
- ¼ cup shredded carrot
- ¼ cup HORMEL® real bacon bits

In small saucepan, combine chicken, mayonnaise, celery, onion, lemon juice, Worcestershire sauce, and pepper. Heat until warm. Place lettuce on toast. Spread chicken mixture over lettuce. Top with shredded carrot and bacon.

Makes 4 servings

• TOASTED COBB SALAD SANDWICH •

GLAZED TERIYAKI CHICKEN STIR–FRY SUB

- ¼ cup *French's*® Honey Dijon Mustard
- 2 tablespoons teriyaki sauce
- 1 tablespoon sucralose sugar substitute
- 1 tablespoon grated, peeled ginger
- 1 tablespoon cider or red wine vinegar
- 1 tablespoon vegetable oil
- 1 pound boneless skinless chicken breasts, cut into thin strips
- 1 cup coarsely chopped red or yellow bell peppers
- ½ cup each coarsely chopped red onion and plum tomatoes
- 2 cups shredded napa cabbage or romaine lettuce
- 4 Italian hero rolls, split (about 8 inches each)

1. Combine mustard, teriyaki sauce, sugar substitute, ginger and vinegar in small bowl; set aside.

2. Heat oil in large skillet or wok over high heat. Stir-fry chicken 5 minutes until no longer pink. Add vegetables and stir-fry 2 minutes until just tender. Pour sauce mixture over stir-fry and cook 1 minute.

3. Arrange cabbage on rolls and top with equal portions of stir-fry. Close rolls. Serve warm.

Makes 4 servings

Prep Time: 10 minutes
Cook Time: 8 minutes

TIP Also known as Chinese cabbage, napa cabbage is easily recognized by its pale green color and crinkled leaves. The mild flavor of its crisp leaves is a perfect addition to this sandwich.

OPEN–FACE CHICKEN SANDWICHES WITH ROASTED PEPPER MAYO

- 4 boneless skinless chicken breasts
- 1 teaspoon dried thyme
- 1 teaspoon garlic salt
- ¼ teaspoon black pepper
- 1 teaspoon olive oil or butter
- ¼ cup mayonnaise
- 3 tablespoons chopped roasted red bell pepper
- 4 slices rye bread, lightly toasted
- 1 cup packed baby spinach

1. Cover chicken breasts with plastic wrap and pound to ⅓-inch thickness. Sprinkle with thyme, garlic salt and black pepper.

2. Heat oil in large nonstick skillet over medium heat. Add chicken; cook 10 to 15 minutes or until no longer pink in center, turning once.

3. Meanwhile, combine mayonnaise and roasted pepper in small bowl until well blended. Spread mayonnaise mixture on bread slices. Top with spinach and chicken.

Makes 4 sandwiches

CHICKEN AND PEAR PITA POCKETS

- 3 cups diced cooked chicken
- 1 can (16 ounces) Bartlett Pear halves or slices, thoroughly drained and diced
- ¾ cup chopped celery
- ½ cup raisins or chopped dates
- ¼ cup *each* plain yogurt and mayonnaise
- 1 teaspoon *each* salt, lemon pepper and dried rosemary leaves, crushed
- 6 pita bread rounds, halved
- 12 lettuce leaves

Combine chicken, pears, celery and raisins in medium bowl. Prepare dressing by blending yogurt, mayonnaise, salt, lemon pepper and rosemary. Combine dressing and pear mixture; mix well. Refrigerate until serving. To serve, line each pita half with lettuce leaf. Portion ½ cup mixture into each half.

Makes 6 servings

Favorite recipe from **Pacific Northwest Canned Pear Service**

• OPEN–FACE CHICKEN SANDWICH WITH ROASTED PEPPER MAYO •

CURRIED CHICKEN SALAD SANDWICHES

- 1 (2- to 3-pound) whole roasted chicken *or* 3½ cups diced cooked chicken
- 1¼ cups halved seedless red grapes
- ½ cup diced Granny Smith apple
- ½ cup toasted sliced almonds
- ⅓ cup golden raisins
- ⅓ cup dried cranberries
- 1 stalk celery, diced
- ¼ cup unsweetened shredded coconut
- ¼ cup finely diced red onion
- ¾ cup mayonnaise
- 1 tablespoon curry powder
- 1 tablespoon fresh lime juice
- 2 teaspoons honey
- Salt and black pepper
- 10 croissants
- 10 red leaf lettuce leaves
- 20 tomato slices

1. Remove skin and bones from chicken; chop meat. Combine chicken, grapes, apple, almonds, raisins, cranberries, celery, coconut and onion in large bowl; set aside.

2. Combine mayonnaise, curry powder, lime juice and honey in medium bowl. Add mayonnaise mixture to chicken mixture; stir until well blended. Season with salt and pepper.

3. Cut croissants in half horizontally. Line bottom halves of croissants with lettuce; top with chicken salad and tomato. Cover with top halves of croissants.

Makes 10 sandwiches

• CURRIED CHICKEN SALAD SANDWICH •

CHICKEN SALSA POCKETS

- 1 can (10¾ ounces) CAMPBELL'S® Condensed Cream of Chicken Soup (Regular or 98% Fat Free)
- ½ cup PACE® Chunky Salsa
- 2 cups cooked chicken, cut into strips
- ½ cup shredded Cheddar cheese
- 3 pita breads (6-inch), cut in half, forming 2 pockets
- Green leaf lettuce leaves

1. Stir the soup, salsa and chicken in a 2-quart saucepan. Cook and stir over medium heat until hot. Stir in the cheese. Cook until the cheese melts.

2. Line the pita halves with lettuce. Spoon about ⅓ cup chicken mixture into each pita half.

Makes 6 sandwiches

Easy Substitution Tip: Substitute 2 cans (4.5 ounces each) SWANSON® Premium Chunk Chicken breast, drained, for the cooked chicken.

Prep/Cook Time: 15 minutes

• CHICKEN SALSA POCKET •

OUP

GRILLED CHICKEN WITH CHIMICHURRI SALSA

4 boneless skinless chicken breasts
½ cup plus 4 teaspoons olive oil, divided
Salt and black pepper
½ cup finely chopped fresh parsley
¼ cup white wine vinegar
2 tablespoons finely chopped onion
3 cloves garlic, minced
1 jalapeño pepper,* finely chopped
2 teaspoons dried oregano

**Jalapeño peppers can sting and irritate the skin, so wear rubber gloves when handling peppers and do not touch eyes.*

1. Prepare grill for direct cooking.

2. Brush chicken with 4 teaspoons oil; season with salt and pepper. Place on grid over medium heat. Grill, covered, 10 to 15 minutes or until no longer pink in center, turning once.

3. For salsa, combine parsley, remaining ½ cup oil, vinegar, onion, garlic, jalapeño pepper and oregano. Season with salt and pepper. Serve salsa over chicken.

Makes 4 servings

CUMIN BBQ CHICKEN

- 1 cup barbecue sauce
- ½ cup orange juice
- 3 tablespoons vegetable oil
- 2 tablespoons minced garlic
- 2 teaspoons ground coriander
- 2 teaspoons ground cumin
- 1 teaspoon black pepper
- ½ teaspoon salt
- 2 whole chickens (about 3½ pounds each), cut up

1. Prepare grill for direct cooking. Combine barbecue sauce, orange juice, oil, garlic, coriander, cumin, pepper and salt in medium bowl; mix well. Reserve ¾ cup sauce.

2. Grill chicken, covered, 20 minutes. Turn and brush with sauce; discard remaining sauce. Grill, covered, 20 minutes or until chicken is cooked through (165°F). Serve with reserved ¾ cup sauce.

Makes 8 servings

CRUNCHY APPLE SALSA WITH GRILLED CHICKEN

- 2 cups Washington Gala apples, halved, cored and chopped
- ¾ cup (1 large) Anaheim chili pepper, seeded and chopped
- ½ cup chopped onion
- ¼ cup lime juice
- Salt and black pepper to taste
- Grilled Chicken (recipe follows)

Combine all ingredients except chicken and mix well; set aside to allow flavors to blend about 45 minutes. Prepare Grilled Chicken. Serve salsa over or alongside Grilled Chicken. *Makes 3 cups salsa*

Grilled Chicken: Marinate 2 whole boneless, skinless chicken breasts in a mixture of ¼ cup dry white wine, ¼ cup apple juice, ½ teaspoon grated lime peel, ½ teaspoon salt and dash pepper for 20 to 30 minutes. Drain and grill over medium-hot coals, turning once, until chicken is no longer pink in center.

Favorite recipe from **Washington Apple Commission**

MEDITERRANEAN CHICKEN KABOBS

- 2 pounds boneless skinless chicken breasts or tenders, cut into 1-inch pieces
- 1 small eggplant, peeled and cut into 1-inch pieces
- 1 medium zucchini, cut into ½-inch slices
- 2 medium onions, each cut into 8 wedges
- 16 mushrooms, stems removed
- 16 cherry tomatoes
- 1 cup chicken broth
- ⅔ cup balsamic vinegar
- 3 tablespoons olive oil
- 2 tablespoons dried mint
- 4 teaspoons dried basil
- 1 tablespoon dried oregano
- 2 teaspoons grated lemon peel
- Chopped fresh parsley
- 4 cups hot cooked couscous

1. Thread chicken, eggplant, zucchini, onions, mushrooms and tomatoes alternately onto 16 metal skewers; place in large glass baking dish.

2. Combine broth, vinegar, oil, mint, basil and oregano in small bowl; pour over kabobs. Cover; marinate in refrigerator 2 hours, turning occasionally. Remove kabobs from marinade; discard marinade.

3. Spray grid with nonstick cooking spray. Prepare grill for direct cooking.

4. Grill kabobs 10 to 15 minutes or until chicken is cooked through, turning once.

5. Stir lemon peel and parsley into couscous; serve with kabobs. *Makes 8 servings*

GRILLED CHICKEN WITH SPICY BLACK BEANS & RICE

2 boneless skinless chicken breasts
1 teaspoon Caribbean jerk seasoning
2 teaspoons olive oil
½ green bell pepper, chopped
2 teaspoons chipotle chili powder
1 cup hot cooked rice
1 cup drained rinsed canned black beans
3 tablespoons chopped pimiento
2 tablespoons chopped pimiento-stuffed green olives
½ small onion, chopped
2 tablespoons chopped fresh cilantro (optional)
Lime wedges (optional)

1. Spray grid with nonstick cooking spray. Prepare grill for direct cooking. Rub chicken with seasoning. Grill over medium-high heat 10 to 15 minutes or until no longer pink in center, turning once.

2. Meanwhile, heat oil in medium saucepan over medium heat. Add bell pepper and chili powder; cook and stir until peppers are tender.

3. Add rice, beans, pimiento and olives to saucepan. Cook about 3 minutes or until heated through.

4. Serve chicken with rice mixture. Sprinkle with onion and cilantro, if desired. Garnish with lime wedges.

Makes 2 servings

TIP Chipotle chili powder is made from red jalapeño peppers that are smoked, dried and ground into a fine powder. It is a convenient way to add rich, smoky flavor and heat to all kinds of dishes. It can be found with other spices in some large supermarkets, as well as in specialty and ethnic markets.

GRILLED CHICKEN TOSTADAS

- 1 pound boneless skinless chicken breasts
- 1 teaspoon ground cumin
- ¼ cup orange juice
- ¼ cup plus 2 tablespoons salsa, divided
- 1 tablespoon plus 2 teaspoons vegetable oil, divided
- 2 cloves garlic, minced
- 8 green onions
- 1 can (16 ounces) refried beans
- 4 (10-inch) or 8 (6-inch) flour tortillas
- 2 cups chopped romaine lettuce
- 1½ cups (6 ounces) shredded Monterey Jack cheese
- 1 ripe avocado, diced
- 1 tomato, seeded and chopped
- Chopped fresh cilantro and sour cream (optional)

1. Place chicken in single layer in shallow glass dish; sprinkle with cumin. Combine orange juice, ¼ cup salsa, 1 tablespoon oil and garlic in small bowl; pour over chicken. Cover; marinate in refrigerator at least 2 hours or up to 8 hours, stirring mixture occasionally.

2. Prepare grill for direct cooking.

3. Drain chicken, reserving marinade. Brush green onions with remaining 2 teaspoons oil. Place chicken and green onions on grid. Grill, covered, over medium-high heat 5 minutes. Brush chicken with half of reserved marinade; turn and brush with remaining marinade. Turn green onions. Grill, covered, 5 minutes or until chicken is no longer pink in center and green onions are tender. (If onions are browning too quickly, remove before chicken is done.)

4. Meanwhile, combine beans and remaining 2 tablespoons salsa in small saucepan; cook and stir over medium heat until heated through.

5. Place tortillas in single layer on grid. Grill, uncovered, 2 to 4 minutes or until golden brown, turning once. (If tortillas puff up, pierce with tip of knife or flatten by pressing with spatula.)

6. Slice chicken crosswise into ½-inch strips. Cut green onions into 1-inch pieces. Spread tortillas with bean mixture; top with lettuce, chicken, green onions, cheese, avocado and tomato. Sprinkle with cilantro and serve with sour cream, if desired.

Makes 4 servings

• GRILLED CHICKEN TOSTADA •

GINGER PEACH BARBECUED CHICKEN

- 2 tablespoons cornstarch
- 1 can (10½ ounces) CAMPBELL'S® Condensed Chicken Broth
- ½ cup peach preserves
- 2 tablespoons dry sherry
- 1 tablespoon soy sauce
- ½ teaspoon ground ginger
- 4½ pounds chicken parts

1. Stir the cornstarch, broth, preserves, sherry, soy and ginger in a 2-quart saucepan. Cook and stir over high heat until the mixture boils and thickens. Remove from the heat. Reserve 1 cup of the broth mixture for barbecue sauce.

2. Lightly oil the grill rack and heat the grill to medium. Grill the chicken for 20 minutes, turning the chicken over halfway through cooking. Grill for 20 minutes more or until chicken is no longer pink, turning and brushing it often with the reserved broth mixture while grilling. Serve the chicken with the remaining broth mixture.

Makes 8 servings

Time-Saving Tip: Barbecue sauce can be made ahead and refrigerated until it's ready to use.

Prep Time: 5 minutes
Grill Time: 45 minutes

SPICY GRILLED CHICKEN THIGHS WITH BLACK–EYED PEA AND MANGO SALSA

- 1 tablespoon olive oil
- 1½ tablespoons fresh lime juice
- ½ teaspoon ground cumin
- 3 to 4 dashes hot sauce or to taste
- 6 boneless skinless chicken thighs
- Salt and black pepper
- Black-Eyed Pea and Mango Salsa (recipe follows)
- Cilantro leaves

Whisk together olive oil, lime juice, cumin and hot sauce in shallow pan. Coat chicken thighs in mixture; season with salt and pepper. Cover and refrigerate at least 30 minutes or several hours. Prepare salsa 1 hour in advance of cooking time.

Preheat charcoal grill. Drain marinade from chicken. Place thighs 4 to 6 inches over medium-hot coals. Cook 3 to 4 minutes on each side or until juices run clear and chicken is no longer pink inside. Serve with salsa. Garnish with cilantro. *Makes 4 to 6 servings*

Favorite recipe from National Chicken Council

BLACK–EYED PEA AND MANGO SALSA

- 16 to 18 red cherry tomatoes (about ½ pound), cut into quarters
- ½ cup cooked black-eyed peas, rinsed and drained
- ½ ripe mango, peeled and diced
- 6 oil-packed sun-dried tomato halves, cut into thin strips
- ¼ cup minced red onion
- 3 tablespoons minced fresh cilantro
- 2 tablespoons fresh lime juice
- 2 tablespoons red wine vinegar
- 2 tablespoons olive oil
- Salt and freshly ground black pepper to taste

Place all ingredients in large bowl; stir gently to combine. Leave at room temperature 1 hour to let flavors develop. Refrigerate leftover salsa. *Makes 4 to 6 servings*

Favorite recipe from National Chicken Council

PESTO–STUFFED GRILLED CHICKEN

2 cloves garlic, peeled
½ cup packed fresh basil leaves
2 tablespoons pine nuts, toasted*
¼ teaspoon black pepper
5 tablespoons extra-virgin olive oil, divided
¼ cup grated Parmesan cheese
1 whole chicken or capon (6 to 7 pounds)
2 tablespoons fresh lemon juice

**To toast pine nuts, spread in single layer on baking sheet. Bake in preheated 350°F oven 8 to 10 minutes or until golden brown, stirring frequently.*

1. Prepare grill for indirect cooking with drip pan in center.

2. For pesto, drop garlic through feed tube of food processor with motor running. Add basil, pine nuts and black pepper; process until basil is minced. With processor running, add 3 tablespoons oil in steady stream until smooth paste forms, scraping down side of bowl once. Add cheese; process until well blended.

3. Remove giblets from chicken cavity; reserve for another use or discard. Loosen skin over breast of chicken by pushing fingers between skin and meat, taking care not to tear skin. Do not loosen skin over wings and drumsticks. Spread pesto under breast skin; massage skin to evenly spread pesto. Combine remaining 2 tablespoons oil and lemon juice in small bowl; brush over chicken skin. Tuck wings under back; tie legs together with wet kitchen string.

4. Place chicken, breast side up, on grid directly over drip pan. Grill, covered, 1 hour 20 minutes or until meat thermometer inserted into thickest part of thigh, not touching bone, registers 165°F.

5. Transfer chicken to carving board; tent with foil. Let stand 15 minutes before carving.

Makes 6 servings

CHIPOTLE ORANGE BBQ DRUMSTICKS

- ½ cup barbecue sauce, preferably mesquite or hickory smoked
- 1 to 2 tablespoons minced canned chipotle peppers in adobo sauce
- 1 teaspoon grated orange peel
- 8 chicken drumsticks
- 1 teaspoon ground cumin

1. Spray grid with nonstick cooking spray. Prepare grill for direct cooking.

2. Combine barbecue sauce, chipotle peppers and orange peel in small bowl.

3. Sprinkle chicken evenly with cumin; grill, covered, over medium-high heat 30 to 35 minutes or until cooked through (165°F), turning frequently. Baste frequently with sauce mixture during last 5 minutes.

Makes 4 servings

CHICKEN ROLL-UPS

- ¼ cup fresh lemon juice
- 1 tablespoon olive oil
- ¼ teaspoon salt
- ¼ teaspoon black pepper
- 4 boneless skinless chicken breasts
- ¼ cup finely chopped fresh parsley
- 2 tablespoons grated Parmesan cheese
- 2 tablespoons chopped fresh chives
- 1 teaspoon grated lemon peel
- 2 cloves garlic, minced

1. Combine lemon juice, oil, salt and pepper in resealable food storage bag. Cover chicken breasts with plastic wrap and pound to ⅜-inch thickness; add to bag. Marinate in refrigerator at least 30 minutes.

2. Prepare grill for direct cooking. Soak 16 toothpicks in warm water 15 minutes.

3. Combine parsley, cheese, chives, lemon peel and garlic in small bowl. Drain chicken; discard marinade. Spread one fourth of parsley mixture over each chicken breast, leaving 1-inch edge. Starting at narrow end, roll chicken to enclose filling; secure with toothpicks.

4. Grill chicken, covered, over medium heat 10 to 15 minutes or until no longer pink in center, turning once. Remove and discard toothpicks before serving.

Makes 4 servings

• CHIPOTLE ORANGE BBQ DRUMSTICK •

LIME–MUSTARD MARINATED CHICKEN

2 boneless skinless chicken breasts
¼ cup fresh lime juice
3 tablespoons honey mustard, divided
2 teaspoons olive oil
¼ teaspoon ground cumin
⅛ teaspoon garlic powder
⅛ teaspoon ground red pepper
¾ cup plus 2 tablespoons chicken broth, divided
¼ cup uncooked rice
1 cup broccoli florets
⅓ cup shredded carrots

1. Place chicken in resealable food storage bag. Whisk together lime juice, 2 tablespoons mustard, oil, cumin, garlic powder and red pepper in small bowl. Pour over chicken. Seal bag; turn to coat. Marinate in refrigerator 2 hours.

2. Spray grid with nonstick cooking spray. Prepare grill for direct cooking.

3. Combine ¾ cup broth, rice and remaining 1 tablespoon mustard in small saucepan. Bring to a boil over high heat. Reduce heat; simmer, covered, 12 minutes or until rice is almost tender. Stir in broccoli, carrots and remaining 2 tablespoons broth. Cover; cook 2 to 3 minutes or until vegetables are crisp-tender and rice is tender.

4. Drain chicken; discard marinade. Grill chicken 10 to 15 minutes or until no longer pink in center, turning once. Serve chicken with rice mixture.

Makes 2 servings

CHICKEN AND VEGETABLE PASTA

- 8 ounces uncooked bowtie pasta
- 1 pound boneless skinless chicken breasts
- 2 red or green bell peppers, cut into quarters
- 1 medium zucchini, cut in half
- ½ cup Italian dressing
- ½ cup prepared pesto

1. Prepare grill for direct cooking.

2. Cook pasta according to package directions. Drain; place in large bowl. Keep warm. Combine chicken, bell peppers, zucchini and dressing in medium bowl; toss well.

3. Grill chicken and vegetables 10 to 15 minutes on each side or until chicken is no longer pink in center, turning once. Cut vegetables and chicken into bite-size pieces. Add chicken, vegetables and pesto to pasta; toss well. *Makes 4 to 6 servings*

BLUE CHEESE STUFFED CHICKEN BREASTS

- 2 ounces crumbled blue cheese
- 2 tablespoons butter, softened, divided
- ¾ teaspoon dried thyme
- Salt and black pepper
- 4 bone-in chicken breasts
- 1 tablespoon fresh lemon juice
- ½ teaspoon paprika

1. Prepare grill for direct cooking. Combine blue cheese, 1 tablespoon butter and thyme in small bowl until blended. Season with salt and pepper.

2. Loosen skin over each chicken breast by pushing fingers between skin and meat, taking care not to tear skin. Spread blue cheese mixture under skin; massage skin to evenly spread cheese mixture.

3. Place chicken, skin side down, on grid over medium heat. Grill, covered, 15 minutes. Meanwhile, melt remaining 1 tablespoon butter; stir in lemon juice and paprika. Turn chicken; brush with lemon juice mixture. Grill 15 to 20 minutes or until chicken is cooked through (165°F). *Makes 4 servings*

SOUTHERN STYLE MUSTARD BBQ CHICKEN KABOBS

- 1½ cups ketchup
- 1 cup prepared mustard
- ½ to ⅔ cup cider vinegar
- ½ cup EQUAL® SPOONFUL*
- 2 tablespoons stick butter or margarine
- 1 tablespoon Worcestershire sauce
- ½ teaspoon maple flavoring
- ½ teaspoon coarsely ground black pepper

**May substitute 12 packets EQUAL® sweetener.*

- 1½ pounds skinless, boneless chicken breasts, cut into ¾-inch cubes
- 2 small yellow summer squash, cut crosswise into 1-inch slices
- 12 medium mushroom caps
- 1 large red or green bell pepper, cut into 1-inch pieces

• Mix all ingredients, except chicken and vegetables, in medium saucepan. Cook over medium heat 3 to 4 minutes or until sauce is hot and butter is melted.

• Assemble chicken cubes and vegetables on skewers; grill over medium heat 10 to 15 minutes until chicken is no longer pink, turning occasionally and basting generously with sauce. Bring remaining sauce to a boil in small saucepan. Boil 5 minutes. Serve with kabobs. *Makes 6 servings*

Tip: Kabobs can also be broiled. Broil 6 inches from heat source until chicken is no longer pink and vegetables are tender, 10 to 12 minutes, turning occasionally and basting generously with sauce. Do not baste during last 5 minutes of broiling.

THAI GRILLED CHICKEN

4 boneless skinless chicken breasts
¼ cup soy sauce
2 teaspoons minced garlic
½ teaspoon red pepper flakes
2 tablespoons honey
1 tablespoon fresh lime juice

1. Prepare grill for direct cooking. Place chicken in shallow baking dish. Combine soy sauce, garlic and pepper flakes. Pour over chicken, turning to coat. Let stand 10 minutes.

2. Combine honey and lime juice in small bowl; blend well.

3. Place chicken on grid over medium heat; brush with marinade. Discard remaining marinade. Grill chicken, covered, 5 minutes. Brush with honey mixture; grill 5 to 10 minutes or until no longer pink in center.

Makes 4 servings

FAJITAS ON A STICK

1¼ pounds boneless, skinless chicken breast halves, cut into 1-inch pieces
1 cup LAWRY'S® Tequila Lime Marinade With Lime Juice
8 wooden skewers, soaked in water for 15 minutes
½ medium onion, sliced into ½-inch slices
½ medium green bell pepper, cut into 1-inch pieces
16 cherry tomatoes
8 flour tortillas (fajita size), warmed

In large resealable plastic bag, combine chicken and ¾ LAWRY'S® Tequila Lime Marinade With Lime Juice; turn to coat. Close bag and marinate in refrigerator 30 minutes. Remove chicken from Marinade, discarding Marinade.

On wooden skewers, alternately thread chicken, onion, pepper and tomatoes. Grill, brushing frequently with remaining ¼ cup Marinade and turning once, 15 minutes or until chicken is thoroughly cooked.

Remove chicken and vegetables from wooden skewer. Roll-up and serve, if desired, with sour cream and shredded cheddar cheese.

Makes 8 fajitas

• THAI GRILLED CHICKEN •

GRILLED LEMON CHICKEN DIJON

- ⅓ cup HOLLAND HOUSE® White with Lemon Cooking Wine
- ⅓ cup olive oil
- 2 tablespoons Dijon mustard
- 1 teaspoon dried thyme
- 2 whole chicken breasts, skinned, boned and halved

In shallow baking dish combine cooking wine, oil, mustard and thyme. Add chicken and turn to coat. Cover; marinate in refrigerator for 1 to 2 hours.

Prepare grill for direct cooking. Drain chicken, reserving marinade. Grill chicken over medium coals 12 to 16 minutes or until cooked through, turning once and basting with marinade.* *Makes 4 servings*

**Do not baste during last 5 minutes of grilling.*

TERIYAKI CHICKEN KABOBS

- ¾ cup teriyaki sauce, divided
- ¼ cup pineapple juice
- 1 teaspoon minced garlic
- 1 pound boneless skinless chicken breasts, cut in 1-inch cubes
- 1 green bell pepper, cut into 1-inch squares
- 2 medium zucchini, cut into ½-inch slices
- 1 red onion, cut into ½-inch chunks
- 1 teaspoon coarsely ground black pepper

1. Combine teriyaki sauce, pineapple juice and garlic. Place chicken in large resealable food storage bag; add ¾ cup teriyaki mixture. Seal bag; turn to coat. Marinate in refrigerator 30 minutes. Reserve remaining marinade.

2. Prepare grill for direct cooking. Soak 6 wooden skewers in water 20 minutes.

3. Drain chicken; discard marinade. Alternately thread chicken, bell pepper, zucchini and onion on skewers; sprinkle with black pepper. Grill 10 to 15 minutes or until chicken is cooked through, turning occasionally and brushing with reserved marinade. *Makes 4 to 6 servings*

MESQUITE–GRILLED CHICKEN QUARTERS

- 2 whole chickens (about 3½ pounds each), cut into quarters
- 2 tablespoons vegetable oil
- 1 small onion, chopped
- 1 clove garlic, minced
- 1 can (12 ounces) beer
- ½ cup tomato juice
- ½ cup ketchup
- ¼ cup Worcestershire sauce
- 2 tablespoons packed brown sugar
- 1 tablespoon fresh lemon juice
- 2 teaspoons chili powder
- 1 teaspoon dry mustard
- ¼ teaspoon salt
- ¼ teaspoon black pepper

1. Preheat oven to 350°F. Place chicken in large baking pan; cover tightly with foil. Bake 30 minutes. Remove foil; cool completely.

2. Heat oil in medium saucepan over medium heat. Add onion and garlic; cook until onion is tender. Combine beer, tomato juice, ketchup, Worcestershire, brown sugar, lemon juice, chili powder, mustard, salt and pepper in medium bowl; whisk until well blended. Pour into saucepan; bring to a boil over high heat. Reduce heat and simmer 20 minutes or until sauce is reduced to about 2 cups, stirring occasionally. Cool completely.

3. Place chicken into 2 large resealable food storage bags. Pour marinade equally over chicken; seal bags. Refrigerate 8 hours or overnight.

4. Spray grid with nonstick cooking spray. Prepare grill for direct cooking. Remove chickens from refrigerator and bring to room temperature.

5. Remove chickens from marinade; reserve marinade. Place marinade in small saucepan; bring to a boil over medium-high heat. Boil 2 minutes. Cool slightly.

6. Hook wing tips back behind body joint on breast pieces of chicken. Place leg and thigh quarters on hottest part of grill; place breasts on cooler edges of grill. Cook, turning occasionally, 20 to 25 minutes or until cooked through (165°F). Brush chicken generously with marinade during the last 10 minutes of cooking.

Makes 8 servings

PERUVIAN GRILLED CHICKEN THIGHS WITH TOMATO–CILANTRO SAUCE

- 8 chicken thighs, bone-in (with or without skin), about 2½ pounds
- 1 teaspoon ground coriander
- ¼ teaspoon cayenne pepper
- ½ teaspoon salt
- 1 ripe avocado, peeled and sliced to garnish
- 2 cups white rice, cooked
- Sour cream

Tomato-Cilantro Sauce

- 2 ripe tomatoes, coarsely chopped
- 1 small red onion, coarsely chopped
- 1 clove garlic, coarsely chopped
- 1 (7-ounce) jar roasted red peppers, drained
- ¼ cup fresh cilantro leaves
- Salt and pepper to taste

Prepare the coals for the grill or preheat the broiler.

In a small bowl, mix together the coriander, cayenne and salt. Rub the chicken thighs with the spice mixture.

Grill the chicken until it is nicely charred all over and the internal temperature is 160°F. when tested with a thermometer.

While the chicken is cooking, prepare the sauce. Put all the sauce ingredients into a blender or food processor and process until smooth. Adjust seasoning and set aside.

To serve, spoon a bed of rice onto each of 4 plates, divide the sauce among them, arrange chicken thighs on top of the sauce and garnish with avocado slices and dollops of sour cream. *Makes 4 servings*

Favorite recipe from National Chicken Council

GRILLED CHICKEN WITH SOUTHERN BARBECUE SAUCE

Nonstick cooking spray
1 small onion, chopped
4 cloves garlic, minced
1 can (16 ounces) tomato sauce
¾ cup water
3 tablespoons packed light brown sugar
3 tablespoons chili sauce
2 teaspoons chili powder
2 teaspoons dried thyme
2 teaspoons Worcestershire sauce
¾ teaspoon ground red pepper
½ teaspoon ground cinnamon
½ teaspoon black pepper
6 bone-in chicken breasts, skinned

1. Spray medium nonstick skillet with cooking spray; heat over medium heat. Add onion and garlic; cook and stir 5 minutes or until tender.

2. Stir in tomato sauce, water, brown sugar, chili sauce, chili powder, thyme, Worcestershire, red pepper, cinnamon and black pepper; bring to a boil over high heat. Reduce heat to low; simmer 30 minutes or until mixture is reduced to about 1½ cups. Reserve ¾ cup sauce; keep remaining sauce warm.

3. Prepare grill for indirect cooking.

4. Grill chicken, covered, 40 to 45 minutes or until cooked through (165°F), turning chicken occasionally and basting with reserved sauce.

5. Serve chicken with remaining warm sauce.

Makes 6 servings

CHICKEN WITH MANGO–CHERRY CHUTNEY

- 1½ cups chopped mango, divided
- ⅓ cup dried cherries
- 1 tablespoon packed brown sugar
- 1 tablespoon cider vinegar
- ½ teaspoon mustard seeds, slightly crushed
- ¼ teaspoon salt, divided
- ¼ cup sliced green onions
- 1½ teaspoons Chinese 5-spice powder
- 4 boneless skinless chicken breasts or 8 boneless skinless chicken thighs

1. Prepare grill for direct cooking.

2. Combine ½ cup mango, cherries, brown sugar, vinegar, mustard seeds and ⅛ teaspoon salt in medium saucepan; cook and stir over medium-low heat 5 minutes or until mango is tender. Slightly mash mango. Stir in remaining 1 cup mango and green onions. Keep warm.

3. Sprinkle chicken with 5-spice powder and remaining ⅛ teaspoon salt; grill 10 to 15 minutes or until no longer pink in center, turning once. Serve chicken with mango mixture. *Makes 4 servings*

HONEY–MUSTARD GRILLED CHICKEN

- 4 boneless skinless chicken breasts (about 4 ounces each)
- ¼ cup honey-mustard salad dressing
- 3 tablespoons grainy Dijon mustard
- 2 tablespoons fresh lemon juice
- 1 tablespoon honey
- Salt and freshly ground black pepper, to taste

In large bowl, whisk salad dressing, mustard, lemon juice, honey, salt and black pepper. Coat chicken halves in mixture. Cover and marinate overnight or at least 15 minutes.

Preheat charcoal grill. Place chicken about 6 inches above medium-hot coals. Grill chicken, turning occasionally, 10 to 20 minutes until juices run clear. *Makes 4 servings*

Tip: Serve with pasta for a quick entrée, toss with greens topped with honey-mustard dressing to make a salad, or melt your favorite cheese slice over for an easy sandwich.

Favorite recipe from **National Chicken Council**

SPICY BARBECUED CHICKEN

- 1 tablespoon paprika or smoked paprika
- 1 teaspoon dried thyme
- ½ teaspoon salt
- ½ teaspoon dried sage
- ¼ teaspoon black pepper
- ¼ teaspoon ground red pepper
- 1 whole chicken (about 3 pounds), quartered
- ¾ cup ketchup
- ½ cup packed brown sugar
- 2 tablespoons soy sauce
- 2 tablespoons Worcestershire sauce
- 1 clove garlic, minced

1. Combine paprika, thyme, salt, sage, black pepper and red pepper in small bowl; sprinkle over chicken. Transfer chicken to resealable food storage bag. Seal bag; refrigerate up to 24 hours.

2. For sauce, combine ketchup, brown sugar, soy sauce, Worcestershire and garlic in medium bowl; mix well. Prepare grill for direct cooking. Grill, covered, 30 to 40 minutes or until cooked through (165°F), turning occasionally. Brush chicken with sauce during last 10 minutes of grilling. *Makes 4 servings*

BOWTIE PASTA WITH GARLIC & GRILLED CHICKEN

- 1 package (16 ounces) uncooked bowtie pasta
- 1¼ pounds boneless skinless chicken breasts
- ¼ cup olive oil
- 4 cloves garlic, minced
- 1½ pounds shiitake mushrooms, sliced
- 2 cups chopped seeded plum tomatoes
- 1 cup chopped green onions
- 1 teaspoon red pepper flakes
- 2 cups chicken broth
- ½ cup chopped fresh cilantro, divided

1. Prepare grill for direct cooking. Cook pasta according to package directions; drain. Keep warm.

2. Grill chicken, covered, 10 to 15 minutes or until no longer pink in center, turning once. Cool slightly. Cut chicken into ½-inch cubes.

3. Heat oil in large skillet over medium heat; cook and stir garlic 1 minute. Add mushrooms, tomatoes, green onions and pepper flakes; cook and stir 2 minutes. Add broth; simmer until slightly reduced. Add chicken and pasta; cook until heated through. Add cilantro; toss to combine. *Makes 6 to 8 servings*

GINGER–LIME CHICKEN THIGHS

6 boneless skinless chicken thighs
⅓ cup vegetable oil
3 tablespoons fresh lime juice
3 tablespoons honey
2 teaspoons grated fresh ginger *or* 1 teaspoon ground ginger
¼ to ½ teaspoon red pepper flakes

1. Place chicken in resealable food storage bag. Combine oil, lime juice, honey, ginger and pepper flakes in small bowl. Add ½ cup marinade to chicken. Seal bag; turn to coat. Marinate in refrigerator 30 to 60 minutes, turning occasionally. Reserve remaining marinade in refrigerator.

2. Prepare grill for direct cooking.

3. Drain chicken; discard marinade. Grill chicken 12 minutes or until cooked through (165°F), turning once. Brush with reserved marinade during last 5 minutes of grilling. *Makes 4 to 6 servings*

LEMON PEPPER CHICKEN

⅓ cup fresh lemon juice
¼ cup finely chopped onion
¼ cup olive oil
1 tablespoon packed brown sugar
1 tablespoon cracked black pepper
3 cloves garlic, minced
2 teaspoons grated lemon peel
¾ teaspoon salt
1 whole chicken (about 3½ pounds), cut into quarters

1. Combine lemon juice, onion, oil, brown sugar, pepper, garlic, lemon peel and salt in small bowl; reserve 2 tablespoons marinade. Combine remaining marinade and chicken in large resealable food storage bag. Seal bag; turn to coat. Refrigerate at least 4 hours or overnight.

2. Prepare grill for direct cooking.

3. Drain chicken; discard marinade. Grill, covered, over medium-high heat 15 to 20 minutes or until cooked through (165°F), turning several times and basting with reserved 2 tablespoons marinade.

Makes 4 servings

• GINGER–LIME CHICKEN THIGHS •

SPICY MANGO CHICKEN

- ¼ cup mango nectar
- ¼ cup chopped fresh cilantro
- 2 jalapeño peppers,* seeded and finely chopped
- 2 teaspoons vegetable oil
- 2 teaspoons LAWRY'S® Seasoned Salt
- ½ teaspoon LAWRY'S® Garlic Powder with Parsley
- ½ teaspoon ground cumin
- 4 boneless, skinless chicken breasts (about 1 pound)
- Mango & Black Bean Salsa (recipe follows)

**Jalapeño peppers can sting and irritate the skin; wear rubber gloves when handling peppers and do not touch eyes.*

In small bowl, combine all ingredients except chicken and salsa; mix well. Brush marinade on both sides of chicken. Grill or broil chicken 10 to 15 minutes or until chicken is thoroughly cooked, turning once and basting often with additional marinade. Do not baste during last 5 minutes of cooking. Discard any remaining marinade. Top chicken with Mango & Black Bean Salsa. *Makes 4 servings*

MANGO & BLACK BEAN SALSA

- 1 ripe mango, peeled, seeded and chopped
- 1 cup canned black beans, rinsed and drained
- ½ cup chopped tomato
- 2 thinly sliced green onions
- 1 tablespoon chopped fresh cilantro
- 1½ teaspoons lime juice
- 1½ teaspoons red wine vinegar
- ½ teaspoon LAWRY'S® Seasoned Salt

In medium bowl, combine all ingredients; mix well. Let stand 30 minutes to allow flavors to blend.
Makes about 2¾ cups

ADOBO GRILLED CHICKEN

- ½ cup chopped onion
- ⅓ cup fresh lime juice
- 6 cloves garlic, coarsely chopped
- 1 teaspoon ground cumin
- 1 teaspoon dried oregano
- ½ teaspoon dried thyme
- ¼ teaspoon ground red pepper
- 6 boneless skinless chicken breasts
- 3 tablespoons chopped fresh cilantro

1. Combine onion, lime juice and garlic in food processor; process until onion is finely minced. Transfer to resealable food storage bag. Add cumin, oregano, thyme and red pepper; knead bag until blended. Add chicken; seal bag. Turn to coat chicken with marinade. Refrigerate 30 minutes or up to 4 hours.

2. Spray grid with nonstick cooking spray. Prepare grill for direct cooking. Drain chicken; discard marinade. Grill, covered, 10 to 15 minutes or until no longer pink in center, turning once. Sprinkle with cilantro.

Makes 6 servings

TIP Adobo is a richly flavored paste of garlic, onion, ground dried chiles and herbs that is used as a marinade or sauce for chicken and pork throughout Latin America and in the Philippines. The presence of an acid, usually vinegar or lime juice, helps to tenderize the meat and adds another dimension of flavor.

CHICKEN AND SPICY BLACK BEAN TACOS

- 1 can (about 15 ounces) black beans, rinsed and drained
- 1 can (10 ounces) diced tomatoes with mild green chiles, drained
- 1 tablespoon plus 1 teaspoon olive oil, divided
- 1½ teaspoons chili powder
- ¾ teaspoon ground cumin
- 12 ounces boneless skinless chicken breasts
- 12 crisp corn taco shells
- Shredded lettuce, diced tomatoes, shredded cheese and sliced black olives (optional)

Slow Cooker Directions

1. Coat slow cooker with nonstick cooking spray. Add beans and tomatoes. Combine 1 teaspoon oil, chili powder and cumin in small bowl; rub all over chicken. Place chicken in slow cooker. Cover; cook on HIGH 1¾ hours.

2. Remove chicken; cool slightly. Cut into thin slices. Transfer bean mixture to bowl using slotted spoon. Stir in remaining 1 tablespoon oil.

3. To serve, warm taco shells according to package directions. Fill with equal amounts bean mixture and chicken. Garnish with lettuce, tomatoes, cheese and olives. *Makes 4 servings*

Prep Time: 10 minutes
Cook Time: 1¾ hours

CHICKEN AND WILD RICE CASSEROLE

- 2 slices bacon, chopped
- 3 tablespoons olive oil
- 1½ pounds chicken thighs
- 1 cup uncooked converted long grain rice
- 6 ounces cremini mushrooms, quartered
- 1 package (4 ounces) uncooked wild rice
- ½ cup diced onion
- ½ cup diced celery
- 2 tablespoons Worcestershire sauce
- ½ teaspoon dried sage
- 3 cups hot chicken broth, or enough to cover chicken
- Salt and black pepper
- 2 tablespoons chopped fresh parsley

Slow Cooker Directions

1. Microwave bacon on HIGH 1 minute. Transfer to slow cooker; drizzle evenly with oil.

2. Place chicken in slow cooker, skin side down. Add long grain rice, mushrooms, wild rice, onion, celery, Worcestershire and sage. Pour broth into slow cooker. Cover; cook on LOW 3 to 4 hours or until rice is tender.

3. Uncover and let stand 15 minutes. Season with salt and pepper. Garnish with parsley.

Makes 4 to 6 servings

Prep Time: 15 minutes
Cook Time: 3 to 4 hours

ASIAN BARBECUE SKEWERS

- 2 pounds boneless skinless chicken thighs
- ½ cup soy sauce
- ⅓ cup packed brown sugar
- 2 tablespoons sesame oil
- 3 cloves garlic, minced
- ½ cup thinly sliced green onions
- 1 tablespoon toasted sesame seeds (optional)

Slow Cooker Directions

1. Cut each thigh into 4 pieces. Thread chicken onto 7-inch-long wooden skewers, folding thinner pieces if necessary. Place skewers in 6-quart slow cooker, layering as flat as possible.

2. Combine soy sauce, brown sugar, oil and garlic in small bowl. Reserve ⅓ cup sauce; set aside. Pour remaining sauce over skewers. Cover; cook on LOW 2 hours. Turn skewers; cook 1 hour or until cooked through.

3. Transfer skewers to serving platter. Discard cooking liquid. Spoon reserved sauce over skewers. Sprinkle with green onions and sesame seeds, if desired. *Makes 4 to 6 servings*

Prep Time: 10 minutes
Cook Time: 3 hours

EASY SLOW COOKER CHICKEN AND GRAVY

- 2 cans (10¾ ounces each) condensed cream of chicken soup, undiluted
- 6 to 8 chicken drumsticks, breasts or assorted pieces

Slow Cooker Directions

Pour 1 can soup into slow cooker. Add chicken. Pour remaining can chicken soup over top. Cover; cook on LOW 8 to 10 hours or until chicken is tender. *Makes 6 servings*

INDIAN–STYLE APRICOT CHICKEN

- 6 chicken thighs
- Salt and black pepper
- 1 tablespoon vegetable oil
- 1 large onion, chopped
- 2 cloves garlic, minced
- 2 tablespoons grated fresh ginger
- ½ teaspoon ground cinnamon
- ⅛ teaspoon ground allspice
- 1 can (about 14 ounces) diced tomatoes
- 1 cup chicken broth
- 1 package (8 ounces) dried apricots
- 1 pinch saffron threads (optional)
- Hot cooked basmati rice
- 2 tablespoons chopped fresh parsley (optional)

Slow Cooker Directions

1. Coat 5-quart slow cooker with nonstick cooking spray. Season chicken with salt and pepper. Heat oil in large skillet over medium-high heat; brown chicken on all sides. Transfer to slow cooker.

2. Add onion to skillet. Cook and stir 3 to 5 minutes or until translucent. Stir in garlic, ginger, cinnamon and allspice. Cook and stir 15 to 30 seconds or until fragrant. Add tomatoes and broth. Cook 2 to 3 minutes or until heated through. Pour into slow cooker.

3. Add apricots and saffron, if desired. Cover; cook on LOW 5 to 6 hours or on HIGH 3 to 3½ hours or until chicken is tender. Season with salt and pepper. Serve with rice; garnish with parsley.

Makes 4 to 6 servings

Prep Time: 15 minutes
Cook Time: 5 to 6 hours (LOW) or 3 to 3½ hours (HIGH)

DIJON CHICKEN THIGHS WITH ARTICHOKE SAUCE

- ⅓ cup Dijon mustard
- 2 tablespoons chopped garlic
- ½ teaspoon dried tarragon
- 2½ pounds chicken thighs, skinned
- 1 cup chopped onion
- 1 cup sliced mushrooms
- 1 jar (12 ounces) quartered marinated artichoke hearts, undrained
- ¼ cup chopped fresh parsley
- Hot cooked fettuccine

Slow Cooker Directions

1. Combine mustard, garlic and tarragon in large bowl. Add chicken thighs and toss to coat. Transfer to 4- to 6-quart slow cooker.

2. Add onion, mushrooms and artichokes with liquid. Cover; cook on LOW 6 to 8 hours or on HIGH 4 hours or until chicken is tender. Stir in parsley just before serving. *Makes 8 servings*

Note: To skin chicken easily, grasp skin with paper towel and pull away. Repeat with fresh paper towel for each piece of chicken, discarding skins and towels.

Prep Time: 10 minutes
Cook Time: 6 to 8 hours (LOW) or 4 hours (HIGH)

NICE 'N' EASY ITALIAN CHICKEN

- 4 boneless skinless chicken breasts (about 1 pound)
- 8 ounces mushrooms, sliced
- 1 medium green bell pepper, chopped
- 1 medium zucchini, diced
- 1 medium onion, chopped
- 1 jar (26 ounces) pasta sauce

Slow Cooker Directions

Layer all ingredients in slow cooker. Cover; cook on LOW 6 to 8 hours or until chicken is tender.
Makes 4 servings

CERVEZA CHICKEN ENCHILADA CASSEROLE

2 cups water
1 stalk celery, chopped
1 small carrot, chopped
1 bottle (12 ounces) Mexican beer, divided
Juice of 1 lime
1 teaspoon salt
1½ pounds boneless skinless chicken breasts
1 can (19 ounces) enchilada sauce
7 ounces corn tortilla chips
½ medium onion, chopped
3 cups shredded Cheddar cheese

Slow Cooker Directions

1. Bring water, celery, carrot, 1 cup beer, lime juice and salt to a boil in large saucepan over high heat; add chicken. Reduce heat; simmer 12 to 14 minutes or until chicken is no longer pink in center. Remove chicken; discard cooking liquid. Cool chicken; shred into bite-size pieces.

2. Spoon ½ cup enchilada sauce into 5-quart slow cooker. Layer tortilla chips over sauce. Cover with one third of shredded chicken and onions. Sprinkle with 1 cup cheese. Spoon ½ cup enchilada sauce over cheese. Repeat layering process 2 more times, pouring remaining beer over casserole before adding last layer of cheese. Cook on LOW 3½ to 4 hours.

Makes 4 to 6 servings

TIP Cooking the chicken breasts in flavorful liquid—in this recipe, a mixture of water, celery, carrot, beer and lime juice—is an easy way to keep the meat juicy and tender. You can also substitute leftover cooked chicken in this recipe for even quicker assembly.

HEARTY CASSOULET

- 1 tablespoon olive oil
- 1 large onion, finely chopped
- 1 pound boneless skinless chicken thighs, chopped
- ¼ pound smoked turkey sausage, finely chopped
- 3 cloves garlic, minced
- 1 teaspoon dried thyme
- ½ teaspoon black pepper
- ¼ cup tomato paste
- 2 tablespoons water
- 3 cans (about 15 ounces each) Great Northern beans, rinsed and drained
- ½ cup plain dry bread crumbs
- 3 tablespoons minced fresh parsley

Slow Cooker Directions

1. Heat oil in large skillet over medium heat. Add onion; cook and stir 5 minutes or until tender. Stir in chicken, sausage, garlic, thyme and pepper. Cook 5 minutes or until chicken and sausage are browned.

2. Remove skillet from heat; stir in tomato paste and water until blended. Place beans and chicken mixture in slow cooker. Cover; cook on LOW 4 to 4½ hours.

3. Just before serving, combine bread crumbs and parsley in small bowl. Sprinkle over cassoulet.

Makes 6 servings

SIMPLE CHICKEN STEW

- 4 to 5 cups chopped cooked chicken (about 5 boneless skinless chicken breasts)
- 1 can (28 ounces) whole tomatoes, cut up, undrained
- 2 large potatoes, cut into 1-inch pieces
- 8 ounces fresh okra, sliced
- 1 large onion, chopped
- 1 can (14 ounces) cream-style corn
- ½ cup ketchup
- ½ cup barbecue sauce

Slow Cooker Directions

Combine chicken, tomatoes, potatoes, okra and onion in slow cooker. Cover; cook on LOW 6 to 8 hours or until potatoes are tender. Add corn, ketchup and barbecue sauce. Cover; cook on HIGH 30 minutes.

Makes 6 servings

MEXICAN BLACK BEAN BOWL

4 chicken thighs, skinned
1 can (about 15 ounces) black beans, rinsed and drained
1 can (about 14 ounces) chicken broth
1 can (about 14 ounces) diced tomatoes with Mexican seasoning or diced tomatoes with green chiles
1 cup finely chopped onion
1 cup frozen corn
1 can (4 ounces) chopped mild green chiles
1 tablespoon chili powder
1 teaspoon ground cumin
1 teaspoon salt
Fried tortilla strips or crushed tortilla chips (optional)

Slow Cooker Directions

1. Coat 4- to 5-quart slow cooker with nonstick cooking spray. Add chicken, beans, broth, tomatoes, onion, corn, chiles, chili powder, cumin and salt. Cover; cook on HIGH 3 to 4 hours.

2. Remove chicken with slotted spoon. Debone and chop chicken. Return to slow cooker and stir well.

3. Serve in bowls. Top with tortilla strips, if desired.

Makes 4 servings

Note: To skin chicken easily, grasp skin with paper towel and pull away. Repeat with fresh paper towel for each piece of chicken, discarding skins and towels.

Prep Time: 10 minutes
Cook Time: 3 to 4 hours

MOROCCAN CHICKEN TAGINE

3 pounds bone-in chicken pieces, skinned
2 cups chicken broth
1 can (about 14 ounces) diced tomatoes
2 onions, chopped
1 cup dried apricots, chopped
6 sprigs fresh cilantro
4 cloves garlic, minced
2 teaspoons ground cumin
1 teaspoon ground cinnamon
1 teaspoon ground ginger
½ teaspoon ground coriander
½ teaspoon ground red pepper
1 tablespoon cornstarch
1 tablespoon water
1 can (about 15 ounces) chickpeas, rinsed and drained
2 tablespoons chopped fresh cilantro
¼ cup toasted slivered almonds
Hot cooked couscous or rice

Slow Cooker Directions

1. Place chicken in 6-quart slow cooker. Combine broth, tomatoes, onions, apricots, cilantro sprigs, garlic, cumin, cinnamon, ginger, coriander and red pepper in medium bowl; pour over chicken. Cover; cook on LOW 4 to 5 hours.

2. Transfer chicken to serving platter; cover and keep warm. Whisk together cornstarch and water in small bowl; add to slow cooker with chickpeas. Cover; cook on HIGH 15 minutes or until sauce is thickened. Pour sauce over chicken. Sprinkle with chopped cilantro and almonds. Serve with couscous.

Makes 4 to 6 servings

Tip: To toast almonds, heat a small nonstick skillet over medium-high heat. Add almonds; cook and stir 3 minutes or until they are just golden brown. Remove from pan immediately. Let almonds cool before adding them to other ingredients.

CREAM CHEESE CHICKEN WITH BROCCOLI

- 4 pounds boneless skinless chicken breasts, cut into ½-inch pieces
- 4 teaspoons olive oil, divided
- 1 package (1 ounce) Italian dressing mix
- 2 cups sliced mushrooms
- 1 cup chopped onion
- 1 can (10¾ ounces) condensed cream of chicken soup, undiluted
- 1 bag (10 ounces) frozen broccoli florets
- 1 package (8 ounces) cream cheese, cubed
- ¼ cup dry sherry

Slow Cooker Directions

1. Combine chicken, 2 teaspoons oil and dressing mix in 5-quart slow cooker, toss to coat. Cover; cook on LOW 3 hours.

2. Heat remaining 2 teaspoons oil in large saucepan over medium heat. Add mushrooms and onion; cook 5 minutes or until tender, stirring occasionally.

3. Add soup, broccoli, cream cheese and sherry to saucepan; cook and stir until heated through. Transfer to slow cooker. Cover; cook on LOW 1 hour.

Makes 10 to 12 servings

CHICKEN AND WILD RICE SOUP

- 3 cans (about 14 ounces each) chicken broth
- 1 pound boneless skinless chicken breasts or thighs, cut into bite-size pieces
- 2 cups water
- 1 cup sliced celery
- 1 cup diced carrots
- 1 package (about 6 ounces) long grain and wild rice mix
- ½ cup chopped onion
- ½ teaspoon black pepper
- 2 teaspoons white vinegar (optional)
- 1 tablespoon chopped fresh parsley

Slow Cooker Directions

1. Combine broth, chicken, water, celery, carrots, rice and seasoning packet, onion and pepper in slow cooker; mix well.

2. Cover; cook on LOW 6 to 7 hours or on HIGH 4 to 5 hours or until chicken is tender. Stir in vinegar, if desired. Sprinkle with parsley.

Makes 8 to 10 servings

GREEK CHICKEN AND ORZO

- 2 medium green bell peppers, cut into thin strips
- 1 cup chopped onion
- 2 teaspoons olive oil
- 8 chicken thighs, skinned
- 1 tablespoon dried oregano
- ½ teaspoon dried rosemary
- ½ teaspoon garlic powder
- 8 ounces uncooked orzo pasta
- ½ cup water
- Grated peel and juice of 1 medium lemon
- Salt and black pepper
- 2 ounces crumbled feta cheese (optional)
- Chopped fresh parsley (optional)

Slow Cooker Directions

1. Coat 6-quart slow cooker with nonstick cooking spray. Add bell peppers and onion.

2. Heat oil in large skillet over medium-high heat. Brown chicken on both sides. Transfer to slow cooker. Sprinkle chicken with oregano, rosemary, and garlic powder. Cover; cook on LOW 5 to 6 hours or on HIGH 3 hours.

3. Transfer chicken to plate; turn slow cooker to HIGH. Stir orzo, water, lemon peel and juice into slow cooker; season with salt and black pepper. Return chicken to slow cooker. Cover; cook 30 minutes or until orzo is tender. Garnish with feta and parsley, if desired. *Makes 4 servings*

Note: To skin chicken easily, grasp skin with paper towel and pull away. Repeat with fresh paper towel for each piece of chicken, discarding skins and towels.

Prep Time: 5 minutes
Cook Time: about 5 to 6 hours (LOW) or about 3½ hours (HIGH)

CHICKEN IN ENCHILADA SAUCE

- 1 can (about 14 ounces) diced tomatoes with chipotle chiles*
- 1 can (10 ounces) enchilada sauce
- 1 cup corn
- ¼ teaspoon ground cumin
- ¼ teaspoon black pepper
- 1½ pounds boneless skinless chicken thighs, cut into bite-size pieces
- 2 tablespoons minced fresh cilantro
- ½ cup shredded pepper jack cheese
- Sliced green onions (optional)

Note: **If tomatoes with chipotle chiles aren't available, use diced tomatoes with green chiles or plain diced tomatoes plus ¼ teaspoon red pepper flakes.**

**If tomatoes with chipotle chiles aren't available, use diced tomatoes with green chiles or plain diced tomatoes plus ¼ teaspoon red pepper flakes.*

Slow Cooker Directions

1. Combine tomatoes, enchilada sauce, corn, cumin and pepper in slow cooker. Add chicken; mix well. Cover; cook on LOW 6 to 7 hours.

2. Stir in cilantro. Spoon chicken and sauce into bowls; sprinkle with cheese and green onions, if desired.

Makes 4 servings

CHICKEN PILAF

- 2 pounds chopped cooked chicken
- 2 cans (8 ounces each) tomato sauce
- 2½ cups water
- 1⅓ cups uncooked long grain converted rice
- 1 cup chopped onion
- 1 cup chopped celery
- 1 cup chopped green bell pepper
- ⅔ cup sliced black olives
- ¼ cup sliced almonds
- ¼ cup (½ stick) butter
- 2 cloves garlic, minced
- 2½ teaspoons salt
- ½ teaspoon ground allspice
- ½ teaspoon ground turmeric
- ¼ teaspoon curry powder
- ¼ teaspoon black pepper

Slow Cooker Directions

Combine all ingredients in slow cooker; stir. Cover; cook on LOW 6 to 8 hours or on HIGH 3 to 4 hours.

Makes 10 servings

• CHICKEN IN ENCHILADA SAUCE •

CHINESE CASHEW CHICKEN

- 1 pound fresh bean sprouts or 1 can (16 ounces) bean sprouts, drained
- 2 cups sliced cooked chicken
- 1 can (10¾ ounces) condensed cream of mushroom soup, undiluted
- 1 cup sliced celery
- ½ cup chopped green onions
- 1 can (4 ounces) sliced mushrooms, drained
- 3 tablespoons butter
- 1 tablespoon soy sauce
- 1 cup whole cashews
- Hot cooked rice

Slow Cooker Directions

1. Combine bean sprouts, chicken, soup, celery, onions, mushrooms, butter and soy sauce in slow cooker; mix well. Cover; cook on LOW 4 to 6 hours or on HIGH 2 to 3 hours.

2. Stir in cashews just before serving. Serve over rice. *Makes 4 servings*

WHITE BEAN CHILI

- Nonstick cooking spray
- 1 pound ground chicken
- 3 cups coarsely chopped celery
- 1 can (28 ounces) whole tomatoes, undrained and coarsely chopped
- 1 can (about 15 ounces) Great Northern beans, rinsed and drained
- 1½ cups coarsely chopped onions
- 1 cup chicken broth
- 3 cloves garlic, minced
- 4 teaspoons chili powder
- 1½ teaspoons ground cumin
- ¾ teaspoon ground allspice
- ¾ teaspoon ground cinnamon
- ½ teaspoon black pepper

Slow Cooker Directions

1. Spray large nonstick skillet with nonstick cooking spray. Brown chicken over medium-high heat, stirring to break up meat.

2. Combine chicken, celery, tomatoes with juice, beans, onions, broth, garlic, chili powder, cumin, allspice, cinnamon and pepper in slow cooker. Cover; cook on LOW 5½ to 6 hours. *Makes 6 servings*

CHICKEN VESUVIO

- 3 tablespoons all-purpose flour
- 1½ teaspoons dried oregano
- 1 teaspoon salt
- ½ teaspoon black pepper
- 1 whole chicken (3 to 4 pounds), cut up, or 3 pounds bone-in chicken pieces
- 2 tablespoons olive oil
- 4 small baking potatoes, scrubbed, cut into 8 wedges each
- 2 small onions, cut into thin wedges
- 4 cloves garlic, minced
- ¼ cup chicken broth
- ¼ cup dry white wine
- ¼ cup chopped fresh parsley
- Lemon wedges (optional)

Slow Cooker Directions

1. Combine flour, oregano, salt and pepper in resealable food storage bag. Add chicken to bag, several pieces at a time; shake to coat lightly with flour mixture.

2. Heat oil in large skillet over medium heat. Add chicken; cook in batches 10 to 12 minutes or until browned on all sides.

3. Place potatoes, onion and garlic in slow cooker. Add broth and wine. Top with chicken pieces; pour pan juices from skillet over chicken. Cover; cook on LOW 6 to 7 hours or on HIGH 3 to 3½ hours or until potatoes are tender.

4. Transfer chicken and vegetables to plates; top with juices from slow cooker. Sprinkle with parsley. Serve with lemon wedges, if desired.

Makes 4 to 6 servings

PROVENÇAL LEMON AND OLIVE CHICKEN

- 2 cups chopped onions
- 8 chicken thighs, skinned
- 1 lemon, thinly sliced and seeds removed
- 1 cup pitted green olives
- 1 tablespoon olive brine from jar or white vinegar
- 2 teaspoons herbes de Provence
- 1 bay leaf
- ½ teaspoon salt
- ⅛ teaspoon black pepper
- 1 cup chicken broth
- ½ cup minced fresh parsley

Slow Cooker Directions

1. Place onions in 4-quart slow cooker. Top with chicken thighs. Place lemon slice on each thigh. Add olives, brine, herbes de Provence, bay leaf, salt and pepper. Slowly pour in broth.

2. Cover; cook on LOW 5 to 6 hours or on HIGH 3 to 3½ hours or until chicken is tender. Stir in parsley before serving.

Makes 8 servings

MILE-HIGH ENCHILADA PIE

- 8 (6-inch) corn tortillas
- 1 jar (12 ounces) salsa
- 1 can (about 15 ounces) kidney beans, rinsed and drained
- 1 cup shredded cooked chicken
- 1 cup shredded Monterey Jack cheese with jalapeño peppers

Slow Cooker Directions

1. Prepare foil handles;* place in slow cooker. Place 1 tortilla in slow cooker. Top with small amount of salsa, beans, chicken and cheese. Continue layering using remaining ingredients, ending with tortilla and cheese.

2. Cover; cook on LOW 6 to 8 hours or on HIGH 3 to 4 hours. Pull out using foil handles. Serve immediately.

Makes 4 to 6 servings

**To make foil handles, tear off 2 (18 × 2-inch) strips of heavy foil or use regular foil folded to double thickness. Crisscross foil strips in spoke design and place in slow cooker to make lifting tortilla stack easier.*

COUNTRY CAPTAIN CHICKEN

- 4 boneless skinless chicken thighs
- 2 tablespoons all-purpose flour
- 2 tablespoons vegetable oil, divided
- 1 cup chopped green bell pepper
- 1 large onion, chopped
- 1 stalk celery, chopped
- 1 clove garlic, minced
- ¼ cup chicken broth
- 2 cups canned crushed tomatoes or diced fresh tomatoes
- ½ cup golden raisins
- 1½ teaspoons curry powder
- 1 teaspoon salt
- ¼ teaspoon paprika
- ¼ teaspoon black pepper
- 2 cups hot cooked rice

Slow Cooker Directions

1. Coat chicken with flour; set aside. Heat 1 tablespoon oil in large skillet over medium-high heat. Add bell pepper, onion, celery and garlic. Cook and stir 5 minutes or until vegetables are tender. Place vegetables in slow cooker.

2. Heat remaining 1 tablespoon oil in same skillet over medium-high heat. Add chicken; brown on both sides. Place chicken in slow cooker.

3. Pour broth into skillet. Cook and stir over medium-high heat, scraping up any browned bits from bottom of skillet; pour into slow cooker. Add tomatoes, raisins, curry powder, salt, paprika and black pepper. Cover; cook on LOW 3 hours. Serve chicken with sauce over rice. *Makes 2 to 4 servings*

ITALIAN CHICKEN WITH SAUSAGE AND PEPPERS

2 tablespoons olive oil
2½ pounds bone-in chicken pieces
½ to ¾ pound sweet Italian sausage
2 green bell peppers, chopped
1 onion, chopped
1 carrot, finely chopped
2 cloves garlic, minced
1 can (15 ounces) tomato sauce
1 can (10¾ ounces) condensed tomato soup, undiluted
¼ teaspoon dried oregano
¼ teaspoon dried basil
1 bay leaf
Salt and black pepper

Slow Cooker Directions

1. Heat oil in large skillet over medium-high heat. Brown chicken 10 minutes, turning once. Transfer chicken to plate.

2. Add sausage to same skillet; brown on all sides. Transfer sausage to plate; cut into 1-inch pieces. Drain off all but 1 tablespoon fat from skillet.

3. Add bell peppers, onion, carrot and garlic to skillet. Cook and stir 4 to 5 minutes or until tender. Add tomato sauce, tomato soup, oregano, basil and bay leaf; stir well. Season with salt and black pepper. Transfer mixture to slow cooker.

4. Add chicken and sausage to slow cooker. Cover; cook on LOW 6 to 8 hours or on HIGH 4 to 6 hours. Remove and discard bay leaf before serving.

Makes 6 servings

SAN MARINO CHICKEN

1 chicken (3 pounds), skinned and cut up
¼ cup all-purpose flour
1 can (8 ounces) tomato sauce
⅓ cup chopped sun-dried tomatoes packed in oil
¼ cup red wine
1 tablespoon grated lemon peel
2 cups sliced mushrooms
2 cups *French's*® French Fried Onions, divided
Hot cooked rice or pasta (optional)

Slow Cooker Directions

1. Lightly coat chicken pieces with flour. Place chicken in slow cooker. Add tomato sauce, sun-dried tomatoes, wine and lemon peel. Cover and cook on LOW setting for 4 hours (or on HIGH for 2 hours).

2. Add mushrooms and *1 cup* French Fried Onions. Cover and cook on LOW setting for 2 hours (or on HIGH for 1 hour) until chicken is no longer pink near bone. Remove chicken to heated platter. Skim fat from sauce.

3. Serve chicken with hot cooked rice or pasta, if desired. Spoon sauce on top and sprinkle with remaining onions. *Makes 4 servings*

Prep Time: 5 minutes
Cook Time: 6 hours (LOW) or 3 hours (HIGH)

PINEAPPLE CHICKEN AND SWEET POTATOES

- ⅔ cup plus 3 tablespoons all-purpose flour, divided
- 1 teaspoon salt
- 1 teaspoon ground nutmeg
- ½ teaspoon ground cinnamon
- ⅛ teaspoon onion powder
- ⅛ teaspoon black pepper
- 6 boneless skinless chicken breasts
- 3 sweet potatoes, peeled and sliced
- 1 can (10¾ ounces) condensed cream of chicken soup, undiluted
- ½ cup pineapple juice
- ¼ pound mushrooms, sliced
- 2 teaspoons packed light brown sugar
- ½ teaspoon grated orange peel
- Hot cooked rice

Slow Cooker Directions

1. Combine ⅔ cup flour, salt, nutmeg, cinnamon, onion powder and pepper in large bowl. Coat chicken with flour mixture. Place sweet potatoes in slow cooker; top with chicken.

2. Combine soup, pineapple juice, mushrooms, remaining 3 tablespoons flour, brown sugar and orange peel in medium bowl; stir well. Pour soup mixture over chicken.

3. Cover; cook on LOW 8 to 10 hours or on HIGH 3 to 4 hours. Serve with rice. *Make 6 servings*

SLOW COOKER CHICKEN CURRY WITH BEER

- ⅓ cup vegetable oil
- 1 whole chicken (about 3½ pounds), cut into 8 pieces
- 1 cup chicken broth
- 1 cup beer
- 1 can (8 ounces) tomato sauce
- 1 large onion, chopped
- 1 tablespoon minced fresh ginger
- 2½ teaspoons curry powder
- 1 teaspoon salt
- 1 teaspoon garam masala
- 2 cloves garlic, minced
- ½ teaspoon chili powder
- Hot cooked basmati rice

Slow Cooker Directions

Heat oil in large skillet over medium-high heat. Cook chicken in batches until browned on all sides. Place chicken into 5-quart slow cooker. Add broth, beer, tomato sauce, onion, ginger, curry powder, salt, garam masala, garlic and chili powder. Cook on LOW 8 hours. Serve over rice. *Makes 4 servings*

CHICKEN AZTECA

- 2 cups frozen corn
- 1 can (about 15 ounces) black beans, rinsed and drained
- 1 cup chunky salsa, divided
- 1 clove garlic, minced
- ½ teaspoon ground cumin
- 4 boneless skinless chicken breasts (about 1 pound)
- 1 package (8 ounces) cream cheese, cubed
- Hot cooked rice
- Shredded Cheddar cheese

Slow Cooker Directions

1. Combine corn, beans, ½ cup salsa, garlic and cumin in slow cooker; top with chicken. Pour remaining ½ cup salsa over chicken. Cover and cook on LOW 4 to 6 hours or on HIGH 2 to 3 hours or until chicken is tender.

2. Remove chicken; cut into bite-size pieces. Return chicken to slow cooker; add cream cheese. Cook on HIGH 10 to 15 minutes or until cream cheese melts and blends into sauce. Serve chicken and sauce over rice. Sprinkle with Cheddar cheese. *Makes 4 servings*

GREEK CHICKEN PITAS WITH CREAMY MUSTARD SAUCE

- 1 medium green bell pepper, cut into ½-inch strips
- 1 medium onion, cut into 8 wedges
- 1 pound boneless skinless chicken breasts
- 1 tablespoon olive oil
- 2 teaspoons Greek seasoning
- ½ teaspoon salt, divided
- ¼ cup plain yogurt
- ¼ cup mayonnaise
- 1 tablespoon prepared mustard
- 4 pita bread rounds
- ½ cup crumbled feta cheese
- Cucumber and tomato slices

Slow Cooker Directions

1. Coat slow cooker with nonstick cooking spray; add bell pepper and onion. Top with chicken and drizzle with oil. Sprinkle evenly with seasoning and ¼ teaspoon salt.

2. Cover; cook on HIGH 1¾ hours or until vegetables are crisp-tender.

3. Remove chicken; thinly slice. Remove pepper and onion using slotted spoon.

4. For sauce, whisk together yogurt, mayonnaise, mustard and remaining ¼ teaspoon salt in small bowl.

5. Warm pitas according to package directions; cut in half. Fill pockets with chicken, pepper, onion, sauce, feta, cucumber and tomato slices.

Makes 4 servings

Prep Time: 10 minutes
Cook Time: 1¾ hours

ZESTY CHICKEN & RICE SUPPER

- 2 boneless skinless chicken breasts, cut into 1-inch pieces
- 2 bell peppers, coarsely chopped
- 1 small onion, chopped
- 1 can (28 ounces) diced tomatoes
- 1 cup uncooked white rice
- 1 cup water
- 1 package (about 1 ounce) taco seasoning mix
- 1 teaspoon salt
- 1 teaspoon black pepper
- 1 teaspoon ground red pepper
- Shredded Cheddar cheese (optional)

Slow Cooker Directions

Layer all ingredients except cheese in slow cooker; mix well. Cover; cook on LOW 6 to 8 hours or on HIGH 3 to 4 hours. Sprinkle with cheese, if desired.

Makes 3 to 4 servings

OLD WORLD CHICKEN AND VEGETABLES

- 1 tablespoon dried oregano
- 1 teaspoon salt, divided
- 1 teaspoon paprika
- ½ teaspoon garlic powder
- ¼ teaspoon black pepper
- 2 green bell peppers, cut into thin strips
- 1 small yellow onion, thinly sliced
- 1 whole chicken, cut into 8 pieces
- ⅓ cup ketchup
- Hot cooked egg noodles

Slow Cooker Directions

1. Combine oregano, ½ teaspoon salt, paprika, garlic powder and black pepper in small bowl; mix well.

2. Place bell peppers and onion in slow cooker. Top with chicken thighs and legs; sprinkle with half of oregano mixture. Top with chicken breasts; sprinkle with remaining oregano mixture. Cover; cook on LOW 8 hours or on HIGH 4 hours. Stir in ketchup and remaining ½ teaspoon salt.

3. Serve chicken and vegetables over noodles.

Makes 4 servings

• ZESTY CHICKEN & RICE SUPPER •

CHICKEN MARSALA WITH FETTUCCINE

- 4 boneless skinless chicken breasts
  Salt and black pepper
- 1 tablespoon vegetable oil
- 1 onion, chopped
- ½ cup marsala wine
- 2 packages (6 ounces each) sliced cremini mushrooms
- ½ cup chicken broth
- 2 teaspoons Worcestershire sauce
- ½ cup whipping cream
- 2 tablespoons cornstarch
- 8 ounces uncooked fettuccine
- 2 tablespoons chopped fresh parsley (optional)

Slow Cooker Directions

1. Coat 5- to 6-quart slow cooker with nonstick cooking spray. Season chicken with salt and pepper; place in slow cooker.

2. Heat oil in large skillet over medium heat. Add onion; cook and stir until translucent. Add marsala; cook 2 to 3 minutes until mixture reduces slightly. Stir in mushrooms, broth and Worcestershire. Pour mixture over chicken. Cover; cook on HIGH 1½ to 1¾ hours.

3. Transfer chicken to cutting board; cool slightly. Whisk cream and cornstarch in small bowl until smooth. Stir into cooking liquid. Cover; cook 15 minutes or until mixture is thickened. Season with salt and pepper.

4. Meanwhile, cook pasta according to directions on package. Drain; transfer to large serving bowl. Slice chicken and place on pasta. Top with sauce and garnish with parsley. *Makes 6 to 8 servings*

Prep Time: 10 minutes
Cook Time: about 2 hours

SOUTH–OF–THE–BORDER CUMIN CHICKEN

- 1 package (16 ounces) frozen bell pepper stir-fry mix, thawed
- 4 chicken drumsticks, skin removed
- 4 chicken thighs, skin removed
- 1 can (about 14 ounces) stewed tomatoes
- 1 tablespoon green pepper sauce
- 2 teaspoons sugar
- 2 teaspoons ground cumin, divided
- 1¼ teaspoons salt
- 1 teaspoon dried oregano
- ¼ cup chopped fresh cilantro
- 1 to 2 medium limes, cut into wedges

Slow Cooker Directions

1. Place bell pepper mix in slow cooker; top with chicken. Combine tomatoes, pepper sauce, sugar, 1 teaspoon cumin, salt and oregano in large bowl. Pour over chicken. Cover; cook on LOW 8 hours or on HIGH 4 hours or until chicken is tender.

2. Place chicken in shallow serving bowl. Stir remaining 1 teaspoon cumin into tomato mixture; pour over chicken. Sprinkle with cilantro. Serve with lime wedges. *Makes 4 servings*

SIMPLE COQ AU VIN

- 1 whole chicken (about 3½ pounds), quartered
- Salt and black pepper
- 2 tablespoons olive oil
- 8 ounces mushrooms, sliced
- 1 onion, cut into rings
- ½ cup red wine
- ½ teaspoon dried basil
- ½ teaspoon dried thyme
- ½ teaspoon dried oregano
- Hot cooked rice

Slow Cooker Directions

1. Season chicken with salt and pepper. Heat oil in large skillet over medium-high heat; brown chicken on all sides. Transfer chicken to slow cooker.

2. Cook and stir mushrooms and onion in same skillet 5 minutes or until tender. Add wine, stirring to scrape up browned bits from bottom of skillet; pour into to slow cooker. Sprinkle with basil, thyme and oregano. Cover; cook on LOW 8 to 10 hours or on HIGH 3 to 4 hours. Serve over rice. *Makes 4 servings*

• SOUTH–OF–THE–BORDER CUMIN CHICKEN •

COUNTRY CHICKEN AND BISCUITS

1 can (10¾ ounces) condensed cream of celery soup, undiluted
⅓ cup milk or water
4 boneless skinless chicken breast halves, cooked and cut into bite-size pieces
1 can (14½ ounces) DEL MONTE® Cut Green Beans, drained
1 can (11 ounces) refrigerated biscuits

1. Preheat oven to 375°F.

2. Combine soup and milk in large bowl. Gently stir in chicken and green beans; season with pepper, if desired. Spoon into 11×7-inch or 2-quart microwavable dish.

3. Cover with plastic wrap; slit to vent. Microwave on HIGH 8 to 10 minutes or until heated through, rotating dish once. If using conventional oven, cover with foil and bake at 375°F, 20 to 25 minutes or until hot.

4. Separate biscuit dough into individual biscuits. Immediately arrange biscuits over hot mixture. Bake in conventional oven about 15 minutes or until biscuits are golden brown and baked through. *Makes 4 servings*

CHEESY CHICKEN ENCHILADAS

¼ cup (½ stick) butter
1 cup chopped onion
2 cloves garlic, minced
¼ cup all-purpose flour
1 cup chicken broth
4 ounces cream cheese, cut into pieces and softened
2 cups (8 ounces) shredded Mexican cheese blend, divided
1 cup shredded cooked chicken
1 can (7 ounces) diced mild green chiles, drained
½ cup diced pimientos
6 (8-inch) flour tortillas, warmed
¼ cup chopped fresh cilantro
¾ cup salsa

1. Preheat oven to 350°F. Spray 13×9-inch baking dish with nonstick cooking spray.

2. Melt butter in medium saucepan over medium heat. Add onion and garlic; cook and stir until onion is tender. Add flour; cook and stir 1 minute. Gradually add broth, stirring constantly. Cook and stir 2 to 3 minutes or until slightly thickened. Add cream cheese; stir until melted. Add ½ cup shredded cheese, chicken, chiles and pimientos; mix well.

3. Spoon about ⅓ cup cheese mixture onto each tortilla. Roll up jelly-roll style and place seam side down in prepared baking dish. Pour remaining cheese mixture over top; sprinkle with remaining 1½ cups shredded cheese.

4. Bake 20 minutes or until bubbly and lightly browned. Sprinkle with cilantro and serve with salsa.

Makes 6 servings

GREEK CHICKEN & SPINACH RICE CASSEROLE

- Nonstick cooking spray
- 1 cup finely chopped onion
- 1 package (10 ounces) frozen chopped spinach, thawed and squeezed dry
- 1 cup uncooked quick-cooking brown rice
- 1 cup water
- ¼ teaspoon salt
- ⅛ teaspoon ground red pepper
- 1 pound chicken tenders
- 2 teaspoons Greek seasoning
- ½ teaspoon lemon pepper
- 1 tablespoon olive oil
- 1 lemon, cut into wedges

1. Preheat oven to 350°F. Spray large ovenproof skillet with cooking spray; heat over medium heat. Add onion; cook and stir 4 minutes or until translucent. Stir in spinach, rice, water, salt and red pepper.

2. Remove skillet from heat; place chicken on top of rice mixture in single layer. Sprinkle with seasoning and lemon pepper. Cover; bake 25 minutes or until chicken is cooked through.

3. Drizzle oil over top of casserole. Serve with lemon wedges. *Makes 4 servings*

CHICKEN VEG•ALL® PARMESAN BAKE

- 1 can (15 ounces) VEG•ALL® Original Mixed Vegetables, undrained
- 1 can cream of celery soup
- 1 can (10 ounces) chunk style white meat chicken, drained
- 2 cups bread crumbs
- ½ cup grated Parmesan cheese, divided

Preheat oven to 350°F.

In mixing bowl, stir together Veg•All with liquid, soup, chicken, bread crumbs and ¼ cup Parmesan cheese.

Spoon into 2-quart casserole dish. Bake 25 to 30 minutes or until edges of mixture are bubbly.

Top with remaining ¼ cup Parmesan cheese. Bake 5 minutes more. Serve hot. *Makes 4 to 6 servings*

CARIBBEAN BRUNCH STRATA

- 6 BAYS® English Muffins, halved, split
- 1 tablespoon Caribbean jerk seasoning (sweet and spicy)
- 1 whole boneless, skinless chicken breast (about 8 ounces), cut into ½-inch pieces
- 1 tablespoon oil
- ¼ cup sliced green onions with tops
- 3 tablespoons flaked or shredded coconut
- 4 ounces mild goat cheese, crumbled
- 6 eggs
- 3¾ cups milk
- ¼ to ½ teaspoon liquid red pepper seasoning
- ½ teaspoon salt
- Mango Salsa (recipe follows)

Preheat oven to 325°F. Arrange half of English muffin pieces on the bottom of a buttered 2-quart glass or porcelain casserole. Sprinkle jerk seasoning on chicken; toss to coat evenly. In a large skillet, heat oil over medium heat. Add chicken; cook and stir until firm, 3 to 5 minutes. Spoon over muffins. Sprinkle with green onions, coconut and goat cheese. Top with remaining muffin pieces. Beat eggs, milk, red pepper seasoning and salt together until blended. Spoon mixture over muffins. Cover with plastic wrap; refrigerate several hours or overnight. When ready to bake, remove plastic. Bake 50 to 60 minutes, until puffy and brown. If necessary, cover with foil during the last 10 minutes of baking to prevent over-browning. Serve with Mango Salsa and tossed green salad. *Makes 4 servings*

MANGO SALSA

- 1 medium mango, peeled, pitted and finely chopped (1 cup)
- 1 red onion, peeled, thinly sliced
- 1 to 2 tablespoons lime juice, to taste
- 1 tablespoon snipped fresh cilantro
- 1 teaspoon minced jalapeño pepper,* seeded and deveined
- ¼ teaspoon freshly grated lime peel
- Salt and black pepper to taste

**Jalapeño peppers can sting and irritate the skin, so wear rubber gloves when handling peppers and do not touch your eyes.*

Combine all ingredients. Cover and refrigerate to blend flavors. *Makes 1 cup salsa*

CHICKEN DIVAN CASSEROLE

Nonstick cooking spray
1 cup uncooked rice
1 cup coarsely shredded carrots
4 boneless skinless chicken breasts
1 pound thawed frozen broccoli florets
2 tablespoons butter
3 tablespoons all-purpose flour
1 cup chicken broth
½ cup milk or half-and-half
¼ cup dry white wine
⅓ cup plus 2 tablespoons grated Parmesan cheese, divided
Salt and black pepper

1. Preheat oven to 350°F. Lightly coat 2-quart baking dish with cooking spray.

2. Prepare rice according to package directions. Stir in carrots. Spread in prepared baking dish.

3. Spray large skillet with cooking spray; heat over medium-high heat. Brown chicken on both sides. Place on top of rice. Arrange broccoli around chicken.

4. Melt butter in medium saucepan over medium heat. Whisk in flour. Gradually whisk in broth and milk. Cook and stir until mixture comes to a boil. Reduce heat; simmer 2 minutes. Stir in wine. Remove from heat; stir in ⅓ cup cheese. Season with salt and pepper; cook and stir 1 minute.

5. Pour sauce over top of casserole; sprinkle with remaining 2 tablespoons cheese. Cover; bake 30 minutes. Uncover; bake 10 minutes or until chicken is no longer pink in center. *Makes 6 servings*

APPLE CURRY CHICKEN

4 boneless skinless chicken breasts
1 cup apple juice, divided
¼ teaspoon salt
Dash black pepper
1½ cups plain croutons
1 medium apple, chopped
1 medium onion, chopped
¼ cup raisins
2 teaspoons packed brown sugar
1 teaspoon curry powder
¾ teaspoon poultry seasoning
⅛ teaspoon garlic powder

1. Preheat oven to 350°F. Lightly grease 2-quart baking dish.

2. Arrange chicken in single layer in prepared baking dish. Combine ¼ cup apple juice, salt and pepper in small bowl; brush over chicken.

3. Combine croutons, apple, onion, raisins, brown sugar, curry powder, seasoning and garlic powder in large bowl. Toss with remaining ¾ cup apple juice; sprinkle over chicken. Cover with foil; bake 45 minutes or until chicken is no longer pink in center. *Makes 4 servings*

SANTA FE CHICKEN & PASTA

1 jar (12 ounces) mild chunky salsa
1 can (10¾ ounces) condensed Cheddar cheese soup
¾ cup sour cream
5 cups hot cooked ziti pasta (8 ounces uncooked)
1⅓ cups *French's*® French Fried Onions, divided
1 package (10 ounces) fully cooked carved chicken breast (2 cups cut-up chicken)
1 cup (4 ounces) cubed Monterey Jack cheese with jalapeño

1. Preheat oven to 375°F. In large bowl, mix salsa, soup and sour cream. Stir in pasta, ⅔ *cup* French Fried Onions, chicken and cheese; mix well. Spoon into 3-quart casserole.

2. Cover; bake 40 minutes or until hot and bubbly. Stir.

3. Sprinkle with remaining ⅔ *cup* onions. Bake 3 minutes or until onions are golden. *Makes 8 servings*

CHICKEN CHILAQUILES WITH SALSA CHIPOTLE

Salsa Chipotle (recipe follows)
12 (6- or 7-inch) corn tortillas
3 teaspoons vegetable oil, divided
2 cups shredded cooked chicken
6 eggs, beaten
1 cup (4 ounces) shredded Monterey Jack cheese
⅓ cup sour cream

1. Prepare Salsa Chipotle. Preheat oven to 375°F. Grease 13×9-inch baking dish.

2. Place all tortillas in single stack on cutting board; cut into thin strips. Heat 1½ teaspoons oil in large skillet over medium-high heat until shimmering. Add half the tortilla strips and fry until golden brown, stirring often to prevent sticking. Transfer with slotted spoon to prepared baking dish. Add remaining 1½ teaspoons oil to skillet; repeat with remaining tortilla strips.

3. Add chicken and Salsa Chipotle to baking dish; toss gently to coat. Stir in eggs. Cover; bake 35 minutes or until center is set. Sprinkle with cheese; bake 5 minutes or until lightly browned. Let stand 15 minutes. Serve with sour cream.

Makes 6 to 8 servings

SALSA CHIPOTLE

1 can (28 ounces) whole tomatoes, drained
2 canned chipotle peppers in adobo sauce
1 tablespoon vegetable oil
½ large white onion, thinly sliced
3 cloves garlic, finely chopped
2½ cups chicken broth
½ cup finely chopped fresh cilantro
Salt

1. Process tomatoes and peppers in food processor using on/off pulsing action until almost smooth.

2. Heat oil in medium saucepan over medium heat. Add onion; cook and stir until golden brown. Add garlic; cook 1 minute. Add tomato mixture; bring to a boil. Reduce heat; simmer 5 minutes or until thickened. Stir in broth. Remove from heat; let cool to room temperature. Add cilantro; season with salt.

Makes 4½ cups

CARMEL CHICKEN FRESCO BAKE

- 4 cups broccoli florets
- 4 tablespoons butter, divided
- 12 ounces cremini mushrooms, sliced
- 3 shallots, diced
- 1 can (14 ounces) artichoke hearts, drained and quartered
- ¼ cup all-purpose flour
- 2½ cups chicken broth
- 1 teaspoon Dijon mustard
- ½ teaspoon salt
- ½ teaspoon dried tarragon
- ½ teaspoon black pepper
- 1 cup (4 ounces) shredded Emmentaler cheese
- 2 pounds boneless skinless chicken breasts, cooked and cut into 1½-inch cubes
- ¼ cup grated Asiago cheese

1. Preheat oven to 350°F. Spray 4-quart baking dish with nonstick cooking spray.

2. Steam broccoli 6 minutes or until tender. Rinse under cold water until cool; drain.

3. Melt 1 tablespoon butter in large skillet over medium heat. Add mushrooms and shallots; cook and stir 5 minutes or until soft. Remove from skillet; combine with broccoli in large bowl. Stir in artichokes.

4. Melt remaining 3 tablespoons butter in same skillet. Add flour, whisking to break up lumps. Add broth, mustard, salt, tarragon and pepper; whisk 2 minutes or until sauce thickens. Add Emmentaler cheese and stir until smooth.

5. Alternately layer chicken and vegetable mixture in baking dish. Pour sauce over top of casserole. Cover with foil; bake 40 minutes. Remove foil; sprinkle with Asiago cheese. Bake 5 minutes or until cheese melts.

Makes 8 servings

CHICKEN CASSOULET

- 4 slices bacon, cut into 1-inch pieces
- ¼ cup all-purpose flour
- Salt and black pepper
- 1¾ pounds bone-in chicken pieces
- 2 chicken sausages, cut into ¼-inch pieces
- 1 medium onion, chopped
- 1 red bell pepper, diced
- 1 green bell pepper, diced
- 2 cloves garlic, finely chopped
- 1 teaspoon dried thyme
- 1 teaspoon olive oil
- 2 cans (about 15 ounces each) cannellini or Great Northern beans, rinsed and drained
- ½ cup dry white wine (optional)

1. Preheat oven to 350°F. Cook bacon in large skillet over medium heat until crisp; drain on paper towels.

2. Pour off all but 2 tablespoons fat from skillet. Place flour in shallow bowl; season with salt and black pepper. Dip chicken in flour mixture, turning to coat; shake off excess flour. Brown chicken in batches in skillet over medium-high heat; transfer to plate. Lightly brown sausages in same skillet; transfer to plate.

3. Add onion, bell peppers, garlic, thyme and oil to skillet. Season with salt and black pepper. Cook and stir over medium heat 5 minutes or until vegetables are softened; transfer to 13×9-inch baking dish. Add beans; mix well. Top with chicken, sausages and bacon.

4. Add wine to skillet, if desired. Cook and stir over medium heat, scraping up browned bits from bottom of skillet; pour over casserole.

5. Cover; bake 40 minutes. Uncover; bake 15 minutes or until chicken is cooked through (165°F).

Makes 6 servings

SMOKY MOUNTAIN CHICKEN AND RICE CASSEROLE

Vegetable oil cooking spray
2 cups sour cream
1 (10¾-ounce) can condensed cream of chicken soup
2 canned chipotle peppers in adobo sauce, finely chopped
1 teaspoon salt
1 teaspoon pepper
3 cups cooked rice
2 cups shredded cooked chicken
2 cups shredded smoked cheddar cheese

Preheat oven to 400°F. Lightly coat 13×9×2-inch baking dish with cooking spray. In large bowl, stir together sour cream, soup, chipotles, salt and pepper until well blended. Stir in rice, chicken and cheese. Spoon into baking dish. Bake uncovered in preheated oven 20 to 25 minutes, until edges of casserole are bubbly. Turn oven to broil setting and lightly brown casserole. *Makes 8 to 10 servings*

Favorite recipe from **USA Rice**

KING RANCH CASSEROLE

1 can (10 ¾ ounces) CAMPBELL'S® Condensed Cream of Mushroom Soup (Regular or 98% Fat Free)
¾ cup PACE® Picante Sauce
¾ cup sour cream
1 tablespoon chili powder
2 medium tomatoes, chopped (about 2 cups)
3 cups cubed cooked chicken or turkey
12 corn tortillas (6-inch), cut into 1-inch pieces
1 cup shredded Cheddar cheese (4 ounces)
Sliced green onions

1. Stir the soup, picante sauce, sour cream, chili powder, tomatoes and chicken in a large bowl.

2. Place half of the tortillas in a 12×8×2-inch shallow baking dish. Top with half the chicken mixture. Repeat the layers. Sprinkle with the cheese.

3. Bake at 350°F. for 40 minutes or until hot. Serve with additional picante sauce and sour cream. Sprinkle with green onions. *Makes 8 servings*

SPICY CHICKEN TORTILLA CASSEROLE

1 tablespoon vegetable oil
1 cup chopped green bell pepper
1 small onion, chopped
2 cloves garlic, finely chopped
1 pound (about 4) boneless, skinless chicken breast halves, cut into bite-size pieces
1 jar (16 ounces) ORTEGA® Salsa, any variety
1 can (2.25 ounces) sliced ripe olives
6 corn tortillas, cut into halves
2 cups (8 ounces) shredded Monterey Jack or cheddar cheese
Sour cream (optional)

PREHEAT oven to 350°F.

HEAT oil in large skillet over medium-high heat. Add bell pepper, onion and garlic; cook for 2 to 3 minutes or until vegetables are tender.

ADD chicken; cook, stirring frequently, for 3 to 5 minutes or until chicken is no longer pink in center. Stir in salsa and olives; remove from heat.

PLACE 6 tortilla halves onto bottom of ungreased 8-inch square baking pan. Top with half of chicken mixture and 1 cup cheese; repeat.

BAKE for 15 to 20 minutes or until bubbly. Serve with sour cream.

Makes 8 servings

HEARTLAND CHICKEN CASSEROLE

- 10 slices white bread, cubed
- 1½ cups plain dry bread crumbs, divided
- 4 cups cubed cooked chicken
- 3 cups chicken broth
- 1 cup chopped onion
- 1 cup chopped celery
- 1 can (8 ounces) sliced mushrooms, drained
- 1 jar (about 4 ounces) pimientos, diced
- 3 eggs, lightly beaten
- Salt and black pepper
- 1 tablespoon butter

1. Preheat oven to 350°F. Combine bread cubes and 1 cup bread crumbs in large bowl. Add chicken, broth, onion, celery, mushrooms, pimientos and eggs; mix well. Season with salt and pepper; spoon into 2½-quart baking dish.

2. Melt butter in small saucepan. Add remaining ½ cup bread crumbs; cook and stir until lightly browned. Sprinkle crumbs over casserole. Bake 1 hour or until bubbly. *Makes 6 servings*

CHICKEN NORMANDY STYLE

- 2 tablespoons butter, divided
- 3 apples, peeled and sliced
- 1 pound ground chicken
- ¼ cup apple brandy or apple juice
- 1 can (10¾ ounces) condensed cream of chicken soup, undiluted
- ¼ cup chopped green onions
- 2 teaspoons fresh minced sage *or* ½ teaspoon dried sage
- ¼ teaspoon black pepper
- 1 package (12 ounces) egg noodles, cooked and drained

1. Preheat oven to 350°F. Grease 9-inch square baking dish.

2. Melt 1 tablespoon butter in 12-inch nonstick skillet over medium heat. Add apples; cook and stir 7 to 10 minutes or until tender. Transfer to plate. Brown chicken in same skillet, stirring to break up meat. Stir in brandy; cook 2 minutes. Stir in soup, green onions, sage, pepper and apples. Reduce heat; simmer 5 minutes.

3. Toss noodles with remaining 1 tablespoon butter. Spoon into prepared baking dish. Top with chicken mixture. Bake 15 minutes or until heated through. *Makes 4 servings*

• HEARTLAND CHICKEN CASSEROLE •

SPICY CHICKEN CASSEROLE WITH CORN BREAD

2 tablespoons olive oil
4 boneless skinless chicken breasts, cut into bite-size pieces
1 package (about 1 ounce) taco seasoning mix
1 can (about 15 ounces) black beans, rinsed and drained
1 can (about 14 ounces) diced tomatoes, drained
1 can (about 10 ounces) Mexican-style corn, drained
1 can (about 4 ounces) diced mild green chiles, drained
½ cup mild salsa
1 box (about 8½ ounces) corn bread mix, plus ingredients to prepare mix
½ cup (2 ounces) shredded Cheddar cheese
¼ cup chopped red bell pepper

1. Preheat oven to 350°F. Spray 2-quart baking dish with nonstick cooking spray.

2. Heat oil in large skillet over medium heat. Cook and stir chicken 3 minutes or until cooked through; sprinkle with seasoning mix. Add beans, tomatoes, corn, chiles and salsa; stir until well blended. Transfer to prepared baking dish.

3. Prepare corn bread mix according to package directions, adding cheese and pepper. Spread batter over chicken mixture. Bake 30 minutes or until corn bread is golden brown. *Makes 6 servings*

TIP Taco seasoning mix is so popular that you will often find a variety to choose from in larger supermarkets, including original, mild, spicy and reduced-sodium versions. Any variety will be great in this casserole so choose the one that works best for you.

CHICKEN, ASPARAGUS & MUSHROOM BAKE

- 1 tablespoon butter
- 1 tablespoon olive oil
- 2 boneless skinless chicken breasts, cut into bite-size pieces
- 2 cloves garlic, minced
- 1 cup sliced mushrooms
- 2 cups sliced asparagus
- Salt and black pepper
- 1 package (about 6 ounces) corn bread stuffing mix
- ¼ cup dry white wine (optional)
- 1 can (about 14 ounces) chicken broth
- 1 can (10¾ ounces) condensed cream of asparagus or cream of chicken soup, undiluted

1. Preheat oven to 350°F. Heat butter and oil in large skillet over medium-high heat until butter is melted. Add chicken and garlic; cook and stir 3 minutes or until chicken is cooked through. Add mushrooms; cook and stir 2 minutes. Add asparagus; cook and stir 5 minutes or until crisp-tender. Season with salt and pepper.

2. Transfer mixture to 2½-quart baking dish or 6 ramekins. Top with stuffing mix.

3. Add wine to skillet, if desired. Cook and stir 1 minute over medium-high heat, scraping up any browned bits from bottom of skillet. Add broth and soup; cook and stir until well blended.

4. Pour broth mixture over stuffing mix; stir gently until blended. Bake 35 minutes (30 minutes for ramekins) or until lightly browned and heated through.

Makes 6 servings

CHICKEN MOLE AND CHEESE PIE

- Cooking Spray
- 1 tablespoon vegetable oil
- 1 tablespoon all-purpose flour
- 1 poblano pepper, seeded, deveined and chopped
- 1 ancho pepper, seeded, deveined and chopped
- 1 green or red bell pepper, seeded, deveined and chopped
- 2 cups chopped onion
- 2 tablespoons brown sugar
- 1½ teaspoons whole cumin seeds
- ½ teaspoon ground coriander
- 1 tablespoon balsamic vinegar
- 1 cup nonfat reduced-sodium chicken broth
- 1 (12-ounce) bottle chili sauce
- 1 ounce unsweetened chocolate, grated
- 4 cups chopped roasted chicken (about 1½ pounds)
- 8 ounces grated CABOT® 50% Reduced Fat Cheddar (about 2 cups)
- 1 (11½-ounce) can refrigerated cornbread twists

1. Preheat oven to 375°F. Coat 12×8-inch baking dish with cooking spray and set aside.

2. Coat large skillet with cooking spray. Add oil, then stir in flour. Place over medium-high heat and stir constantly until mixture turns light brown, about 3 minutes. Add peppers and onion; cook, stirring constantly, until tender. Stir in brown sugar, cumin seeds and coriander; cook, stirring constantly, for 2 minutes longer. Stir in vinegar, scraping to loosen any browned bits from bottom of skillet.

3. Add chicken broth, chili sauce and chocolate to skillet; cook, stirring frequently, until thickened, about 10 minutes. Fold in chicken.

4. Spoon mixture evenly into prepared dish. Sprinkle evenly with cheese.

5. Unroll cornbread dough, separating into strips. Place strips in lattice fashion over chicken mixture. Bake for 15 minutes, or until lattice is golden brown. Let stand for 15 minutes before serving.

Makes 10 servings

MOROCCAN CHICKEN, APRICOT & ALMOND CASSEROLE

1 pound ground chicken
¾ teaspoon salt, divided
¼ teaspoon ground cinnamon
¼ teaspoon black pepper
1 tablespoon olive oil
1 small onion, chopped
1 cup sliced dried apricots
1 can (28 ounces) diced tomatoes
½ teaspoon ground ginger
½ teaspoon red pepper flakes
1 can (10½ ounces) condensed chicken broth
½ cup water
1 cup large-pearl couscous*
¼ cup toasted sliced almonds

**Large-pearl couscous, also known as Israeli couscous, is the size of barley and is available in many supermarkets. If it is not available, substitute small-grain couscous.*

1. Preheat oven to 325°F. Grease 11×7-inch baking dish.

2. Combine chicken, ½ teaspoon salt, cinnamon and black pepper in medium bowl. Shape into 1-inch balls.

3. Heat oil in large skillet over medium heat. Add meatballs; brown on all sides. Transfer to plate. Add onion and apricots to skillet. Cook 5 minutes or until onion is tender. Stir in tomatoes, ginger, pepper flakes and remaining ¼ teaspoon salt; simmer 5 minutes.

4. Meanwhile, bring broth and water to a boil in small saucepan. Stir in couscous. Reduce heat; cover and simmer 10 minutes or until couscous is tender and almost all liquid has been absorbed. Drain if necessary.

5. Spoon couscous into prepared baking dish. Top with meatballs; spoon tomato mixture over meatballs. Bake 20 minutes or until meatballs are cooked through. Sprinkle with almonds. *Makes 4 to 6 servings*

Note: To cook small-grain couscous, follow package directions using 1 cup chicken broth in place of water. Remove from heat and let stand 5 minutes or until all liquid is absorbed. Fluff with a fork.

CHICKEN POT PIE

- 1½ pounds bone-in chicken pieces, skinned
- 1 cup chicken broth
- ½ teaspoon salt
- ¼ teaspoon black pepper
- 1 to 1½ cups milk
- 3 tablespoons butter
- 1 medium onion, chopped
- 1 cup sliced celery
- ⅓ cup all-purpose flour
- 2 cups frozen mixed vegetables, thawed
- 1 teaspoon dried parsley flakes
- ½ teaspoon dried thyme
- 1 (9-inch) refrigerated pastry crust
- 1 egg, lightly beaten

1. Bring chicken, broth, salt and pepper to a boil in large saucepan over medium-high heat. Reduce heat to low. Cover; simmer 30 minutes or until chicken is cooked through (165°F). Remove chicken; let cool.

2. Pour chicken broth mixture into measuring cup; add enough milk to equal 2½ cups. Remove chicken from bones and cut into ½-inch pieces.

3. Melt butter in same saucepan over medium heat. Add onion and celery; cook and stir 3 minutes. Stir in flour until well blended. Gradually stir in broth mixture; cook, stirring constantly, until thickened. Add chicken, vegetables, parsley and thyme. Pour into 1½-quart deep casserole.

4. Preheat oven to 400°F. Roll out pastry to 1 inch larger than diameter of casserole on lightly floured surface. Cut slits in pastry to vent; place on top of casserole. Roll edges and cut away extra pastry; flute edges. Roll scraps to cut into decorative designs and place on top of pastry, if desired. Brush pastry with egg. Bake 30 minutes until crust is golden brown and filling is bubbly.

Makes 4 servings

Note: You can substitute 2 cups diced cooked chicken and 1 can (about 14 ounces) chicken broth for the first two ingredients. In Step 2, combine broth with enough milk to equal 2½ cups. Proceed with recipe.

SAFFRON CHICKEN & VEGETABLES

- 2 tablespoons vegetable oil
- 6 chicken thighs, skinned
- 1 bag (16 ounces) frozen mixed vegetables, such as broccoli, red bell peppers, mushrooms and onions, thawed
- 1 can (about 14 ounces) chicken broth
- 1 can (10¾ ounces) condensed cream of chicken soup, undiluted
- 1 can (10¾ ounces) condensed cream of mushroom soup, undiluted
- 1 package (about 5 ounces) uncooked saffron yellow rice mix
- ½ cup water
- 1 teaspoon paprika (optional)

Preheat oven to 350°F. Spray 3-quart baking dish with nonstick cooking spray. Heat oil in large skillet over medium heat. Brown chicken on both sides. Combine vegetables, broth, soups, rice mix and water in large bowl; mix well. Place mixture in prepared casserole. Top with chicken. Sprinkle with paprika, if desired. Cover; bake 1½ hours or until chicken is cooked through (165°F). *Makes 6 servings*

CRANBERRY CHICKEN VEG•ALL® CASSEROLE

- 1 box (6.7 ounces) brown and wild rice mix
- 2½ cups water
- 1 cup cooked chicken, cubed
- ¾ cup chopped walnuts
- ½ cup dried cranberries
- ¼ cup Marsala wine, optional
- 1 tablespoon grated orange zest
- 1 tablespoon butter
- 1 can (15 ounces) VEG•ALL® Original Mixed Vegetables, drained
- Salt and pepper, to taste
- ⅓ cup goat cheese, crumbled (optional)

Microwave Directions

Combine the first eight ingredients in a 2 quart casserole dish. Cover and microwave on HIGH 10 minutes.

Stir in Veg•All, cover and microwave an additional 10 to 15 minutes or until rice is cooked and liquid is absorbed. Season to taste with salt and pepper.

Cover and let stand 5 minutes. Sprinkle with goat cheese, if desired. *Makes 5 cups*

CHICKEN FLORENTINE LASAGNA

- 2 cans ($10\frac{3}{4}$ ounces each) CAMPBELL'S® Condensed Cream of Chicken with Herbs Soup
- 2 cups milk
- 1 egg
- 1 container (15 ounces) ricotta cheese
- 6 uncooked lasagna noodles
- 1 package (about 10 ounces) frozen chopped spinach, thawed and well drained
- 2 cups cubed cooked chicken or turkey
- 2 cups shredded Cheddar cheese (8 ounces)

1. Stir the soup and milk with a whisk or spoon in a medium bowl.

2. Stir the egg and ricotta cheese in a small bowl.

3. Spread 1 cup of the soup mixture in a 13×9×2-inch shallow baking dish. Top with 3 of the lasagna noodles, ricotta mixture, spinach, chicken, 1 cup of the Cheddar cheese and 1 cup of the soup mixture. Top with remaining 3 lasagna noodles and remaining soup mixture. Cover the dish with foil.

4. Bake at 375°F. for 1 hour. Uncover the dish and top with the remaining Cheddar cheese. Let the lasagna stand for 5 minutes before serving.

Makes 6 servings

Time-Saving Tip: To thaw spinach, microwave on HIGH for 3 minutes, breaking apart with a fork halfway through heating.

Prep Time: 10 minutes
Bake Time: 1 hour

CAJUN CHICKEN AND RICE

- 4 chicken drumsticks, skin removed
- 4 chicken thighs, skin removed
- 2 teaspoons Cajun seasoning
- ¾ teaspoon salt
- 2 tablespoons vegetable oil
- 1 can (about 14 ounces) chicken broth
- 1 cup uncooked rice
- 1 green bell pepper, coarsely chopped
- 1 red bell pepper, coarsely chopped
- ½ cup finely chopped green onions
- 2 cloves garlic, minced
- ½ teaspoon dried thyme
- ¼ teaspoon ground turmeric

1. Preheat oven to 350°F. Lightly coat 13×9-inch baking dish with nonstick cooking spray; set aside.

2. Sprinkle chicken with seasoning and salt. Heat oil in large skillet over medium-high heat. Add chicken; cook 8 to 10 minutes or until browned on all sides. Transfer to plate.

3. Add broth to skillet. Bring to a boil, stirring to scrape up browned bits. Stir in rice, peppers, green onions, garlic, thyme and turmeric. Pour into prepared baking dish; top with chicken. Cover; bake 1 hour or until chicken is cooked through (165°F).

Makes 6 servings

TIP For easier clean up, skip the baking dish and use an ovenproof skillet instead. Simply place the browned chicken on top of the rice mixture in the skillet then cover and bake as directed.

GREEN CHILE–CHICKEN CASSEROLE

4 cups shredded cooked chicken
1½ cups green enchilada sauce
1 can (10¾ ounces) condensed cream of chicken soup, undiluted
1 container (8 ounces) sour cream
1 can (4 ounces) diced mild green chiles
½ cup vegetable oil
12 (6-inch) corn tortillas
1½ cups (6 ounces) shredded Mexican cheese blend, divided

1. Preheat oven to 325°F. Grease 13×9-inch baking dish. Combine chicken, enchilada sauce, soup, sour cream and chiles in large skillet. Cook and stir over medium-high heat until warm.

2. Heat oil in separate large deep skillet. Fry tortillas just until crisp; drain on paper towels. Place 4 tortillas on bottom of prepared baking dish. Layer with one third of chicken mixture and ½ cup cheese. Repeat layers twice. Bake 15 to 20 minutes or until heated through. *Makes 6 servings*

SPLIT–BISCUIT CHICKEN PIE

⅓ cup butter
⅓ cup all-purpose flour
2½ cups milk
1 tablespoon chicken bouillon granules
½ teaspoon dried thyme
½ teaspoon black pepper
4 cups diced cooked chicken
2 jars (4 ounces each) diced pimientos, drained
1 cup frozen peas, thawed
1 package (6 ounces) refrigerated biscuits

1. Preheat oven to 350°F. Coat 2-quart baking dish with nonstick cooking spray.

2. Melt butter in large skillet over medium heat. Add flour; whisk until smooth. Add milk, bouillon, thyme and pepper; whisk until smooth. Cook and stir until thickened. Remove from heat. Stir in chicken, pimientos and peas. Pour mixture into prepared baking dish. Bake 30 minutes.

3. Meanwhile, bake biscuits according to package directions. Split biscuits in half; arrange cut side down on top of chicken mixture. Bake 3 minutes or until biscuits are heated through. *Makes 6 servings*

SESAME CHICKEN

1 pound boneless skinless chicken breasts or thighs
⅔ cup teriyaki sauce, divided
2 teaspoons cornstarch
1 tablespoon peanut or vegetable oil
2 cloves garlic, minced
2 green onions, cut into ½-inch slices
1 tablespoon sesame seeds, toasted*
1 teaspoon dark sesame oil

**To toast sesame seeds, spread seeds in small skillet. Cook and stir over medium-low heat 3 minutes or until seeds begin to pop and turn golden.*

1. Cut chicken into 1-inch pieces; toss with ⅓ cup teriyaki sauce in medium bowl. Marinate at room temperature 15 minutes or cover and refrigerate up to 2 hours.

2. Drain chicken; discard marinade. Blend remaining ⅓ cup teriyaki sauce into cornstarch in small bowl until smooth.

3. Heat peanut oil in large deep skillet or wok over medium-high heat. Add chicken and garlic; stir-fry 3 minutes or until chicken is cooked through. Stir cornstarch mixture; add to skillet. Cook and stir 1 minute or until sauce boils and thickens. Stir in green onions, sesame seeds and sesame oil.

Makes 4 servings

HERB ROASTED CHICKEN

- 1 whole chicken (about 3½ pounds)
- 1¼ teaspoons salt, divided
- ½ teaspoon black pepper, divided
- 1 lemon, cut into quarters
- 4 sprigs fresh rosemary, divided
- 4 sprigs fresh thyme, divided
- 4 cloves garlic, peeled
- 2 tablespoons olive oil

1. Preheat oven to 425°F. Place chicken, breast side up, in shallow roasting pan. Season cavity of chicken with ½ teaspoon salt and ¼ teaspoon pepper. Fill cavity with lemon quarters, 2 sprigs rosemary, 2 sprigs thyme and garlic cloves.

2. Chop leaves from remaining 2 rosemary and thyme sprigs. Combine with oil, remaining ¾ teaspoon salt and ¼ teaspoon pepper in small bowl. Brush mixture over chicken.

3. Roast chicken 30 minutes. Reduce oven temperature to 375°F; roast 35 to 45 minutes or until cooked through (165°F). Let stand 10 to 15 minutes before carving. *Makes 4 servings*

CREAMY CURRY LEMON CHICKEN

- ½ cup sour cream
- ¼ cup mayonnaise
- 2 tablespoons fresh lemon juice
- 1 teaspoon curry powder
- ½ teaspoon sugar
- ½ teaspoon salt
- ½ teaspoon black pepper
- 4 boneless skinless chicken breasts
- 1 cup plain dry bread crumbs

1. Preheat oven to 400°F. Grease 2-quart baking dish.

2. Combine sour cream, mayonnaise, lemon juice, curry powder, sugar, salt and pepper in small bowl; stir until well blended.

3. Place chicken in prepared baking dish. Spoon sour cream mixture evenly over chicken. Sprinkle with bread crumbs. Bake 30 to 40 minutes or until chicken is no longer pink in center. *Makes 4 servings*

CHICKEN BROCCOLI ROULADE WITH PARMESAN CREAM SAUCE

Parmesan Cream Sauce (recipe follows)
4 boneless skinless chicken breasts
Salt and black pepper
1 tablespoon olive oil
1 pound broccoli, cut into thin florets
2 cloves garlic, minced
¼ cup grated Parmesan cheese
1 tablespoon butter
Chopped fresh parsley (optional)

1. Prepare Parmesan Cheese Sauce; keep warm.

2. Place plastic wrap over chicken breasts and pound to ¼-inch thickness. Season with salt and pepper.

3. Heat oil in 12-inch skillet over medium heat. Add broccoli and garlic; cook 5 minutes or until crisp-tender. Remove from heat; add Parmesan cheese. Let stand 5 minutes.

4. Wrap broccoli with chicken, securing with toothpicks, if necessary.

5. Melt butter in same skillet over medium-high heat. Add chicken; cook 10 minutes or until no longer pink in center, turning once. Remove toothpicks; serve with sauce. Sprinkle with parsley, if desired.

Makes 4 servings

PARMESAN CREAM SAUCE

2 tablespoons butter
2 teaspoons flour
¾ cup whipping cream
½ cup grated Parmesan cheese

Melt butter in large skillet over medium-high heat. Add flour; cook 1 minute, whisking constantly. Add cream; cook 2 minutes, whisking until thickened and smooth. Reduce heat to low. Add Parmesan cheese, stirring until smooth.

Makes 4 servings

CHICKEN FAJITAS

- 1 pound chicken tenders
- ¼ cup fresh lime juice
- 4 cloves garlic, minced, divided
- Nonstick cooking spray
- 1 cup sliced red bell peppers
- 1 cup sliced green bell peppers
- 1 cup sliced yellow bell peppers
- 1 onion, sliced
- ½ teaspoon ground cumin
- ¼ teaspoon salt
- ¼ teaspoon ground red pepper
- 8 teaspoons sour cream
- 8 (6-inch) flour tortillas, warmed
- Salsa (optional)

1. Place chicken, lime juice and half of garlic in medium bowl; toss to coat. Cover; marinate in refrigerator 30 minutes, stirring occasionally.

2. Spray large nonstick skillet with cooking spray; heat over medium heat. Add chicken mixture; cook and stir 5 to 7 minutes or until no longer pink in center.

3. Add bell peppers, onion and remaining garlic to skillet; cook and stir 5 minutes or until tender. Sprinkle with cumin, salt and red pepper. Return chicken to skillet. Cook and stir 1 to 2 minutes or until heated through.

4. Spread 1 teaspoon sour cream on each tortilla. Spoon chicken and bell pepper mixture over sour cream; roll up tortillas. Serve with salsa, if desired. *Makes 4 servings*

SWEET AND SOUR CHICKEN

- ¼ cup chicken broth
- 2 tablespoons soy sauce
- 2 tablespoons hoisin sauce
- 1 tablespoon cider vinegar
- 1 tablespoon tomato paste
- 2 teaspoons packed brown sugar
- 1 clove garlic, minced
- ¼ teaspoon black pepper
- 1 pound boneless skinless chicken thighs, cut into 1-inch pieces
- 2 teaspoons cornstarch
- 2 tablespoons minced fresh chives
- Hot cooked rice

Slow Cooker Directions

1. Combine broth, soy sauce, hoisin sauce, vinegar, tomato paste, brown sugar, garlic and pepper in 4-quart slow cooker; mix well. Add chicken thighs; toss to coat. Cover; cook on LOW 2½ to 3½ hours.

2. Blend cornstarch into 2 tablespoons cooking liquid in measuring cup until smooth; add to slow cooker. Stir in chives. Turn heat to HIGH. Cook and stir 2 minutes or until sauce is slightly thickened. Serve chicken and sauce over rice. *Makes 4 servings*

VENETIAN CHICKEN WITH CREAMY PESTO SAUCE

- 1 tablespoon olive oil
- 1 red or yellow bell pepper, cut into chunks
- 1 pound boneless skinless chicken breasts or thighs, cut into 1-inch chunks
- ½ teaspoon salt
- ¼ teaspoon black pepper
- ½ cup half-and-half
- ½ cup prepared pesto
- 3 cups hot cooked spaghetti or vermicelli pasta (6 ounces uncooked)
- ¼ cup grated Asiago or Parmesan cheese

1. Heat oil in large nonstick skillet over medium heat. Add bell pepper; cook and stir 3 minutes. Add chicken, salt and black pepper; cook and stir 5 minutes.

2. Add half-and-half and pesto; cook 3 minutes or until chicken is cooked through and bell pepper is tender, stirring occasionally. Serve over pasta; sprinkle with cheese. *Makes 4 servings*

JERK CHICKEN AND PASTA

- Jerk Sauce (recipe follows)
- 1 pound boneless skinless chicken breasts
- Nonstick cooking spray
- 1 green bell pepper, sliced
- 1 cup chicken broth
- 2 green onions, sliced
- 8 ounces fettuccine, cooked and drained
- Grated Parmesan cheese (optional)

1. Prepare Jerk Sauce. Spread sauce on both sides of chicken. Cover and refrigerate 15 to 30 minutes.

2. Spray medium skillet with cooking spray; heat over medium heat. Add chicken; cook 10 minutes or until no longer pink in center. Add bell pepper, broth and green onions; bring to a boil. Reduce heat and simmer 5 to 7 minutes or until vegetables are crisp-tender.

3. Remove chicken from skillet. Let stand 5 minutes; cut into slices. Toss fettuccine, chicken and vegetable mixture in large serving bowl. Sprinkle with Parmesan cheese. *Makes 4 servings*

JERK SAUCE

- ¼ cup loosely packed fresh cilantro
- 2 tablespoons coarsely chopped fresh ginger
- 2 tablespoons black pepper
- 2 tablespoons fresh lime juice
- 3 cloves garlic
- 1 tablespoon ground allspice
- ½ teaspoon curry powder
- ¼ teaspoon ground cloves
- ⅛ teaspoon ground red pepper

Combine all ingredients in food processor or blender; process until thick paste forms.

Makes about ¼ cup

HONEY–MUSTARD CHICKEN WITH APPLES

- 4 boneless skinless chicken breasts
- 1 medium green apple, cored and cut into 8 wedges
- Salt and black pepper
- ¾ cup peach jam
- 1 red bell pepper, diced
- 2 tablespoons honey mustard
- 1 tablespoon cornstarch
- 1 clove garlic, minced
- ½ teaspoon ground ginger
- ¼ cup sliced green onions

1. Prepare grill for direct cooking. Spray 4 (18×12-inch) pieces heavy-duty foil with nonstick cooking spray.

2. Place 1 chicken breast and 2 apple wedges in center of each sheet foil; season with salt and black pepper.

3. Combine jam, bell pepper, mustard, cornstarch, garlic and ginger in small bowl. Spoon over chicken and apples.

4. Double-fold sides and ends of foil to seal packets, leaving head space for heat circulation. Place on baking sheet.

5. Slide packets onto grid. Grill, covered, 11 to 13 minutes until chicken is no longer pink in center. Carefully open one end of each packet to allow steam to escape. Open packets and transfer mixture to serving plates. Sprinkle with green onions before serving. *Makes 4 servings*

MOROCCAN CHICKEN WITH APRICOT COUSCOUS

- 4 boneless, skinless chicken breast halves
- ½ teaspoon garlic salt
- ¼ teaspoon allspice
- ⅛ teaspoon cayenne pepper
- 1 tablespoon olive oil
- ¼ cup apricot preserves
- 2 teaspoons lemon juice
- Apricot Couscous (recipe follows)

In small dish, mix together garlic salt, allspice and cayenne pepper; sprinkle over chicken. In nonstick frypan, heat oil to medium-high temperature. Add chicken and cook, turning, about 10 minutes or until chicken is brown. Reduce heat to medium-low, cover and cook 5 minutes or until chicken is fork tender. Stir in apricot preserves and lemon juice. Heat until preserves melt; spoon glaze over chicken. Place Apricot Couscous on serving platter; top with chicken and glaze. *Makes 4 servings*

Apricot Couscous: In medium nonstick frypan, heat 2 teaspoons olive oil over medium heat. Add ¼ cup chopped dried apricots, ¼ cup raisins, ¼ cup chopped English walnuts and 1 finely minced garlic clove; cook, stirring, about 3 minutes or until garlic is tender. Add 2 cups cooked couscous; heat through. Serve with Moroccan Chicken. Makes 4 servings.

Favorite Recipe from **Delmarva Poultry Industry, Inc.**

CHICKEN WITH HERBED CHEESE

- 4 boneless skinless chicken breasts
- 1 tablespoon butter
- 2 cups chopped shiitake mushrooms
- 1 large shallot, minced
- ¼ teaspoon dried thyme
- ½ teaspoon salt, divided
- ½ teaspoon black pepper, divided
- ¼ cup half-and-half
- ¼ cup chicken broth
- ¼ cup garlic-and-herb spreadable cheese
- 4 thin slices ham
- 1 tablespoon minced fresh parsley

1. Preheat oven to 350°F. Place plastic wrap over chicken breasts and pound to ¼-inch thickness.

2. Melt butter in medium skillet over medium heat. Add mushrooms, shallot, thyme, ¼ teaspoon salt and ¼ teaspoon pepper; cook 5 minutes or until mushrooms are tender. Add half-and-half and broth; simmer 5 minutes or until slightly thickened. Pour half of mixture into shallow baking dish.

3. Spread 1 tablespoon cheese down center of each breast. Top with 1 ham slice; roll up. Place chicken, seam side down, in baking dish. Sprinkle with remaining ¼ teaspoon salt and pepper. Top with remaining mushroom mixture. Bake 20 to 25 minutes or until chicken is cooked through (165°F). Sprinkle with parsley.

Makes 4 servings

CORNISH HENS WITH WILD RICE AND PINE NUT PILAF

- 1/3 cup uncooked wild rice
- 4 Cornish hens (about 1 1/4 pounds each)
- 1 bunch green onions, cut into 2-inch pieces
- 3 tablespoons olive oil, divided
- 3 tablespoons soy sauce
- 1/3 cup pine nuts
- 1 cup chopped onion
- 1 teaspoon dried basil
- 2 garlic cloves, minced
- 2 jalapeño peppers,* seeded and minced
- 1/2 teaspoon salt
- Black pepper (optional)

***Jalapeño peppers can sting and irritate the skin; wear rubber gloves when handling peppers and do not touch eyes. Wash hands after handling.**

1. Preheat oven to 425°F. Cook rice according to package directions.

2. Place hens on rack in roasting pan. Stuff with equal amounts of green onions; roast 15 minutes. Meanwhile, combine 1 tablespoon oil and soy sauce in small bowl; reserve 2 tablespoons soy sauce mixture. Baste hens with remaining soy sauce mixture; roast 15 minutes or until cooked through (165°F). Baste with reserved 2 tablespoons soy sauce mixture. Let stand 15 minutes.

3. Heat large skillet over medium-high heat; add pine nuts. Cook and stir 2 minutes or until golden. Transfer to plate; cool completely.

4. Add 1 tablespoon oil to same skillet; heat 30 seconds. Add onion and basil; cook 5 minutes or until browned, stirring frequently. Add garlic; cook and stir 15 seconds. Remove from heat; add rice, pine nuts, jalapeño peppers, remaining 1 tablespoon oil and salt. Season with black pepper, if desired; toss gently to blend. Serve hens with rice mixture.

Makes 4 servings

SPICY GRITS WITH CHICKEN

- 4 cups chicken broth
- 1 cup grits
- 1 jalapeño pepper,* seeded and finely chopped
- ½ teaspoon salt
- ¼ teaspoon paprika
- ¼ teaspoon black pepper
- ¾ cup (3 ounces) shredded sharp Cheddar cheese
- 1½ cups chopped cooked chicken
- ½ cup half-and-half
- 2 tablespoons chopped fresh chives

**Jalapeño peppers can sting and irritate the skin, so wear rubber gloves when handling peppers and do not touch eyes.*

Slow Cooker Directions

1. Combine broth, grits, jalapeño pepper, salt, paprika and black pepper in slow cooker. Cover; cook on LOW 4 hours.

2. Add cheese and stir until melted. Stir in chicken, half-and-half and chives. Cover; cook on LOW 15 minutes. Serve immediately.

Makes 6 servings

Prep Time: 10 minutes
Cook Time: about 4 hours

TIP Though most people associate grits with corn, they can actually be any grain that is coarsely ground. Delicious, inexpensive and versatile, grits can be served all day long. At breakfast, you'll find them lightly sweetened and served as a hot cereal. At dinner, they find their savory side in hearty side dishes or as part of an easy main course like this one.

SPANISH BRAISED CHICKEN WITH GREEN OLIVES AND RICE

- 2 pounds chicken thighs, skinned
- 1 teaspoon paprika
- Nonstick cooking spray
- ¾ cup dry sherry
- 2¼ cups water
- 1 can (about 14 ounces) chicken broth
- ¾ cup sliced pimiento-stuffed green olives
- 1½ teaspoons dried sage
- 1½ cups uncooked long grain white rice

1. Sprinkle chicken with paprika. Spray large nonstick skillet with cooking spray; heat over medium-high heat. Cook chicken 6 to 8 minutes or until golden brown, turning once. Transfer to plate.

2. Add sherry to same skillet, stirring to scrape up browned bits. Add water, broth, olives and sage; bring to a boil. Reduce heat to low. Return chicken to skillet. Cover; simmer 10 minutes.

3. Add rice to skillet; gently stir to distribute evenly. Cover; simmer 20 to 25 minutes or until liquid is absorbed and rice is tender. *Makes 6 servings*

APRICOT OLIVE CHICKEN

- 1 teaspoon olive oil
- 4 chicken legs
- 1 teaspoon paprika
- 3 tablespoons sliced garlic
- 1 tablespoon chopped rosemary
- ¼ cup marsala wine
- 1½ cups low-sodium chicken broth
- 1 cup dried apricots
- 1 cup sliced California Ripe Olives

Heat oil in a large high-sided sauté pan over medium-high heat. Season chicken legs with salt and place in pan, skin side down. Cook for 3 to 4 minutes until browned, then turn over. Sprinkle with paprika, stir in garlic and rosemary and continue cooking for 1 to 2 more minutes, then add marsala wine.

Pour in chicken broth, apricots and California Ripe Olives and bring to a boil. Turn heat down to low, cover and simmer for 1½ hours until chicken is fork-tender. *Makes 4 servings*

Favorite recipe from **California Olive Industry**

ITALIAN CHICKEN SAUTÉ

2 tablespoons olive or vegetable oil
1 pound boneless, skinless chicken breast halves, cut into strips
½ cup chopped green bell pepper
½ cup chopped onion
1 large clove garlic, minced
1 cup sliced fresh mushrooms
2 medium zucchini, sliced (about 1 cup)
1 can (14.5 ounces) CONTADINA® Recipe Ready Diced Tomatoes, undrained
2 tablespoons capers
1 tablespoon chopped fresh basil or 1 teaspoon dried basil leaves, crushed
½ teaspoon Italian herb seasoning
¼ teaspoon salt
⅛ teaspoon crushed red pepper flakes
1 tablespoon cornstarch

1. Heat oil in large skillet. Add chicken, bell pepper, onion and garlic; sauté for 3 to 4 minutes or until chicken is lightly browned.

2. Add mushrooms and zucchini; sauté for 2 to 3 minutes or until zucchini are crisp-tender.

3. Drain tomatoes, reserving juice in small bowl. Add tomatoes, capers, basil, Italian seasoning, salt and red pepper flakes to skillet.

4. Add cornstarch to reserved tomato juice; mix well. Stir into mixture in skillet. Cook, stirring constantly, until liquid is thickened. Serve over hot cooked rice, if desired. *Makes 4 servings*

Prep Time: 12 minutes
Cook Time: 13 minutes

CHICKEN CORDON BLEU

- 4 boneless skinless chicken breasts
- ¼ cup all-purpose flour
- 1 teaspoon paprika
- ½ teaspoon salt
- ¼ teaspoon black pepper
- 4 slices ham
- 4 slices Swiss cheese
- 2 tablespoons olive oil
- ½ cup white wine
- ½ cup chicken broth
- ½ cup half-and-half
- 2 tablespoons cornstarch

Slow Cooker Directions

1. Place plastic wrap over chicken breasts and pound to ½-inch thickness. Combine flour, paprika, salt and pepper in resealable food storage bag; shake well.

2. Place 1 slice ham and 1 slice cheese on each breast; roll up. Secure with toothpicks. Add to bag; shake gently to coat with flour mixture.

3. Heat oil in large skillet over medium-high heat. Add chicken; brown on all sides. Transfer to 4-quart slow cooker. Remove skillet from heat; add wine, stirring to scrape up browned bits. Pour into slow cooker. Add broth. Cover; cook on LOW 2 hours.

4. Remove chicken with slotted spoon; cover and keep warm. Combine half-and-half and cornstarch in small bowl until smooth; add to slow cooker. Cover; cook on LOW 15 minutes or until sauce has thickened. Remove toothpicks before serving; serve with sauce. *Makes 4 servings*

Prep Time: 20 minutes
Cook Time: 2 hours

COCOA–COFFEE SPICED CHICKEN WITH SALSA MOLE

2 tablespoons ground coffee
2 tablespoons HERSHEY®'S Cocoa
1 tablespoon salt
1 tablespoon brown sugar
4 boneless, skinless chicken breasts
1 tablespoon vegetable oil
1 teaspoon chili powder
Salsa Mole (recipe follows)
Cilantro sprigs (optional)
Black beans (optional)
Rice (optional)

1. Heat oven to 425°F. Grease baking sheet.

2. Stir together coffee, cocoa, salt, brown sugar and chili powder. Rub chicken pieces with vegetable oil; pat on cocoa mixture. Place coated chicken pieces on prepared baking sheet.

3. Bake 20 to 25 minutes or until juices are clear. Meanwhile, prepare Salsa Mole.

4. Arrange chicken and salsa on large platter. Garnish with cilantro sprigs, if desired. Serve with black beans and rice, if desired.

Makes 4 servings

SALSA MOLE

2 tomatoes, chopped
1 avocado, peeled and diced
1 green onion, minced
1 tablespoon snipped cilantro
1 clove garlic, pressed
¼ cup HERSHEY®'S Mini Chips Semi-Sweet Chocolate
1 teaspoon lime juice

Stir together tomatoes, avocado, onion, cilantro, garlic, small chocolate chips and lime juice in medium bowl.

Makes about 2 cups

CHICKEN AND HERB STEW

- ½ cup all-purpose flour
- ½ teaspoon salt
- ¼ teaspoon paprika
- ¼ teaspoon black pepper
- 4 chicken drumsticks
- 4 chicken thighs
- 2 tablespoons olive oil
- 12 ounces new potatoes, quartered
- 2 medium carrots, quartered lengthwise and cut into 3-inch pieces
- 1 green bell pepper, cut into thin strips
- ¾ cup chopped onion
- 2 cloves garlic, minced
- 1¾ cups water
- ¼ cup dry white wine
- 2 chicken bouillon cubes
- 1 tablespoon chopped fresh oregano
- 1 teaspoon chopped fresh rosemary leaves
- 2 tablespoons chopped fresh parsley (optional)

1. Combine flour, salt, paprika and black pepper in shallow dish; stir until well blended. Coat chicken evenly with flour mixture; shake off excess.

2. Heat oil in large skillet over medium-high heat. Brown chicken on all sides. Transfer to plate.

3. Add potatoes, carrots, bell pepper, onion and garlic to same skillet. Cook and stir 5 minutes or until vegetables are lightly browned. Add water, wine and bouillon, stirring to scrape up browned bits. Add oregano and rosemary.

4. Arrange chicken on top of vegetable mixture, turning several times to coat. Cover tightly; simmer 45 to 50 minutes or until chicken is cooked through (165°F). Garnish with parsley. *Makes 4 servings*

GREEK CHICKEN AND ARTICHOKE RICE

- 2 tablespoons olive oil, divided
- 1 pound chicken tenders
- Paprika
- ¼ cup pine nuts
- 2 cups chicken broth
- 1 can (14 ounces) artichoke hearts, drained and quartered
- 1 cup uncooked rice
- 1½ tablespoons grated lemon peel
- 1 clove garlic, minced
- ½ teaspoon salt, divided
- ⅛ teaspoon black pepper
- Juice of 1 medium lemon
- 2 tablespoons chopped fresh parsley
- 2 ounces feta cheese with sun-dried tomatoes and basil, crumbed

1. Heat 1 tablespoon oil in large skillet over medium-high heat. Sprinkle chicken lightly with paprika. Place in skillet and cook 2 minutes on one side. Transfer to plate.

2. Add pine nuts to same skillet; cook 1 minute or until golden brown, stirring constantly. Stir in broth, artichokes, rice, lemon peel, garlic, ¼ teaspoon salt and pepper. Return chicken to skillet, seasoned side up; press down gently into rice mixture. Bring to a boil. Reduce heat; cover and simmer 15 minutes or until rice is tender.

3. Remove from heat; drizzle with lemon juice and remaining 1 tablespoon oil. Sprinkle with parsley, feta cheese and remaining ¼ teaspoon salt. Do not stir. Serve immediately. *Makes 4 servings*

ROAST CHICKEN WITH SPICED MUSHROOM AND WINTER VEGETABLE STUFFING

Chicken

- 1 (5-pound) roasting chicken
- ¼ teaspoon salt
- ¼ teaspoon freshly ground pepper
- 1 tablespoon butter
- ¼ teaspoon ground cinnamon
- ¼ teaspoon ground cumin
- ¼ teaspoon ground coriander
- ½ cup chicken broth
- ¾ cup dry sherry
- 1 tablespoon all-purpose flour

Stuffing

- 1 tablespoon butter
- 1 medium onion, finely chopped
- ¼ teaspoon ground cinnamon
- ¼ teaspoon ground cumin
- ¼ teaspoon ground coriander
- 8 ounces mushrooms, finely chopped
- 1 cup coarsely grated parsnips
- 1 cup coarsely grated carrots
- 1 cup bread crumbs, lightly toasted
- ½ cup finely chopped hazelnuts, lightly toasted
- ½ cup chicken broth
- ⅛ teaspoon salt
- ⅛ teaspoon freshly ground pepper
- Additional all-purpose flour

Preheat oven to 400°F.

Rinse chicken under cold running water; drain. Salt and pepper inside of chicken cavity. Melt 1 tablespoon butter and add ¼ teaspoon each of cinnamon, cumin and coriander. Brush mixture over chicken. Tie up legs securely with butcher's string; place chicken on rack set in roasting pan. Add ½ cup chicken broth. Roast for 30 minutes.

While chicken is roasting, in large saucepan over medium heat, melt 1 tablespoon butter. Stir in onion and sauté for 5 minutes, until translucent. Stir in spices; cook about 1 minute, until aroma is released. Add mushrooms, parsnips and carrots; cook until all vegetables are tender and any excess liquid has evaporated, about 6 minutes. Remove from heat; stir in bread crumbs, hazelnuts and ½ cup chicken broth. Add salt and pepper. Place in ceramic or glass casserole dish.

Reduce oven temperature to 350°F. Place stuffing in oven and continue to roast chicken for another 1 hour 15 minutes, until meat thermometer registers 180°F when inserted between thigh and breast. Check roasting pan periodically as chicken cooks; if pan becomes dry, add water, several tablespoons at a time.

When done, remove chicken to serving platter and cover with foil.

Skim fat off juices left in roasting pan. Set pan over low heat; add sherry, stirring to scrape up any bits of chicken stuck to pan. Stir in small amount of flour to thicken slightly; simmer about 1 minute.

Pour pan juices into gravy boat or small pitcher. Uncover chicken; remove string from legs; carve and serve with gravy and stuffing.

Makes 6 servings

Favorite recipe from **National Chicken Council**

CHICKEN RUSTIGO

- 4 boneless skinless chicken breast halves
- 1 package (10 ounces) fresh mushrooms, sliced
- ¾ cup chicken broth
- ¼ cup dry red wine or water
- 3 tablespoons *French's*® Spicy Brown Mustard
- 2 plum tomatoes, coarsely chopped
- 1 can (14 ounces) artichoke hearts, drained and quartered
- 2 teaspoons cornstarch

1. Season chicken with salt and pepper. Heat *1 tablespoon* oil in large nonstick skillet over medium-high heat. Cook chicken 5 minutes or until browned on both sides. Remove and set aside.

2. Heat *1 tablespoon* oil in same skillet over medium-high heat until hot. Add mushrooms. Cook and stir 5 minutes or until mushrooms are tender. Stir in broth, wine and mustard. Return chicken to skillet. Add tomatoes and artichoke hearts. Heat to boiling. Reduce heat to medium-low. Cook, covered, 10 minutes or until chicken is no longer pink in center.

3. Combine cornstarch and *1 tablespoon* cold water in small bowl. Stir into skillet. Heat to boiling. Cook, stirring, over high heat about 1 minute or until sauce thickens. Serve with hot cooked orzo pasta, if desired.

Makes 4 servings

Prep Time: 10 minutes
Cook Time: 21 minutes

CHICKEN AND RED PEPPERS WITH PARMESAN PENNE

8 ounces uncooked penne pasta
2 tablespoons olive oil, divided
4 boneless skinless chicken breasts
1 medium onion, chopped
2 teaspoons minced garlic
1 tablespoon flour
½ cup chicken broth
1 jar (about 12 ounces) roasted red peppers, drained and chopped
¾ cup grated Parmesan cheese, divided
¼ cup half-and-half
Salt and black pepper

1. Cook pasta according to package directions; drain. Keep warm.

2. Meanwhile, heat 1 tablespoon oil in large skillet over medium-high heat. Brown chicken on both sides. Cover and cook 10 minutes or until no longer pink in center, turning once. Transfer to plate; keep warm.

3. Heat remaining 1 tablespoon oil in same skillet over medium heat. Add onion; cook and stir 3 minutes or until translucent. Add garlic; cook and stir 1 minute. Add flour; stir until smooth. Add broth; cook and stir until slightly thickened. Stir in pasta, roasted peppers, ½ cup Parmesan cheese and half-and-half. Season with salt and black pepper. Top with chicken; cover and simmer 5 to 10 minutes or until heated through. Sprinkle with remaining ¼ cup Parmesan cheese. Serve immediately.

Makes 4 servings

CHICKEN WITH RICE & ASPARAGUS PILAF

- 4 boneless skinless chicken breasts
- 3 teaspoons poultry seasoning, divided
- 2 tablespoons olive oil
- 1 medium onion, chopped
- 1 cup uncooked rice
- 1 clove garlic, minced
- 2 cups chicken broth
- ¾ teaspoon salt
- 1 pound asparagus, cut into 2-inch pieces (about 3 cups)

1. Sprinkle chicken with 1 teaspoon seasoning. Heat oil in large skillet over medium-high heat. Brown chicken on both sides. Transfer to plate.

2. Add onion to same skillet; cook and stir 3 minutes. Add rice and garlic; cook and stir 1 minute. Add broth, remaining 2 teaspoons seasoning and salt. Bring to a boil over high heat. Reduce heat to low; simmer, covered, 5 minutes. Stir in asparagus and chicken. Simmer, covered, 10 to 12 minutes or until rice is tender and chicken is no longer pink in center. *Makes 4 servings*

CHICKEN FRIED RICE

- 1 bag SUCCESS® Rice
- ½ pound boneless skinless chicken breasts, cut into ½-inch pieces
- ½ teaspoon salt
- ¼ teaspoon pepper
- 2 tablespoons vegetable oil
- 1 clove garlic, minced
- ½ teaspoon grated fresh ginger
- 2 cups sliced green onions
- 1 cup sliced fresh mushrooms
- 2 tablespoons reduced-sodium soy sauce
- 1 teaspoon sherry
- 1 teaspoon Asian-style hot chili sesame oil (optional)

Prepare rice according to package directions.

Sprinkle chicken with salt and pepper; set aside. Heat vegetable oil in large skillet over medium-high heat. Add garlic and ginger; cook and stir 1 minute. Add chicken; stir-fry until no longer pink in center. Add green onions and mushrooms; stir-fry until tender. Stir in soy sauce, sherry and sesame oil. Add rice; heat thoroughly, stirring occasionally. *Makes 6 servings*

• CHICKEN WITH RICE & ASPARAGUS PILAF •

CHICKEN WELLINGTON

- 6 boneless skinless chicken breasts
- ¾ teaspoon salt, divided
- ¼ teaspoon black pepper, divided
- 4 tablespoons butter, divided
- 12 ounces button or cremini mushrooms, finely chopped
- ½ cup finely chopped shallots or onion
- 2 tablespoons port wine or cognac
- 1 tablespoon minced fresh thyme *or* 1 teaspoon dried thyme
- 1 package (about 17 ounces) frozen puff pastry, thawed
- 1 egg, separated
- 1 tablespoon Dijon mustard
- 1 teaspoon milk

1. Sprinkle chicken with ¼ teaspoon salt and ⅛ teaspoon pepper. Melt 2 tablespoons butter in large skillet over medium heat. Brown chicken on both sides, working in batches. Transfer to plate; let cool.

2. Melt remaining 2 tablespoons butter in same skillet over medium heat. Add mushrooms and shallots; cook and stir 5 minutes or until mushrooms release their liquid. Add wine, thyme, remaining ½ teaspoon salt and ⅛ teaspoon pepper; simmer 3 minutes or until liquid evaporates, stirring often. Let cool.

3. Roll out each pastry sheet to 15×12-inch rectangle. Cut each into 3 (12×5-inch) rectangles. Cut small amount of pastry from corners into decorative shapes; set aside. Lightly beat egg white; brush over pastry rectangles. Place 1 chicken breast on 1 side of each pastry rectangle. Spread ½ teaspoon mustard over each chicken breast, then spread with ¼ cup mushroom mixture. Fold pastry over chicken, pressing edges to seal. Place on ungreased baking sheet; top with pastry shapes. Whisk egg yolk and milk in small bowl; brush over pastry. Cover loosely with plastic wrap. Refrigerate until cold, 1 to 4 hours.

4. Preheat oven to 400°F. Bake 25 to 30 minutes or until chicken is cooked through (165°F) and pastry is golden brown.

Makes 6 servings

CHICKEN PROSCIUTTO ROLLS

1 can (28 ounces) tomato sauce
2 cloves garlic, minced
1 teaspoon dried oregano
1 teaspoon dried basil
4 boneless skinless chicken breasts
8 slices prosciutto
1 jar (12 ounces) roasted red peppers, drained and halved
1 cup grated Asiago cheese, divided
Hot cooked spaghetti

1. Preheat oven to 350°F. Combine tomato sauce, garlic, oregano and basil in medium bowl. Spoon 1 cup sauce into 3-quart baking dish; reserve remaining sauce.

2. Slice each chicken breast in half crosswise to make 8 thin pieces. Place plastic wrap over chicken pieces and pound to ¼-inch thickness.

3. Place prosciutto slice, 1 roasted pepper half and 1 tablespoon cheese on each piece of chicken. Roll up, starting from long side. Place rolls, seam side down, in prepared baking dish. Pour reserved sauce over chicken.

4. Cover; bake 50 minutes or until chicken is no longer pink in center. Sprinkle with remaining ½ cup cheese. Bake, uncovered, 10 minutes or until cheese is melted. Slice chicken rolls; serve with sauce over spaghetti.

Makes 4 servings

TIP You will find both imported and domestic prosciutto in the deli section of large supermarkets and Italian specialty markets. Prosciutto di Parma is typically the most expensive, followed by imports from other areas, with domestic options being the least expensive.

CHICKEN WITH GARLIC SAUCE

- Nonstick cooking spray
- 4 boneless skinless chicken breasts
- Salt and black pepper
- ¼ cup all-purpose flour
- ¼ cup olive oil
- 1½ cups thinly sliced onions
- 1 green bell pepper, cut into thin strips
- 4 cloves garlic, minced
- 1 can (14 ounces) chicken broth
- 3 cups hot cooked rice

1. Coat large skillet with nonstick cooking spray; heat over medium-high heat. Season chicken with salt and black pepper; brown 2 minutes on one side. Transfer to plate.

2. Reduce heat to medium. Add flour and oil to skillet; cook and stir 3 minutes or until flour begins to brown. Add onions, bell pepper and garlic; cook and stir 6 minutes or until onions are translucent.

3. Add broth; bring to a boil. Add chicken and any juices; return to a boil. Reduce heat; cover and simmer 15 minutes or until chicken is no longer pink in center. Serve over rice. *Makes 4 servings*

SCALLOPINI WITH CAPERS, LEMON AND ARTICHOKE

- 2 tablespoons all-purpose flour
- Salt and pepper, to taste
- ½ (16-ounce) package PERDUE® Fit 'N Easy® Thin-Sliced Skinless & Boneless Chicken Breast or Turkey Breast Cutlets
- 2 tablespoons olive oil
- 1 (14-ounce) can artichoke hearts in water, drained and chopped
- 2 tablespoons capers, chopped
- 1½ tablespoons lemon juice
- 2 tablespoons chopped parsley
- 2 tablespoons butter

In a shallow dish, stir together the flour, salt and pepper. Coat chicken slices on both sides with flour mixture, patting off excess. Warm olive oil in a large, non-stick skillet over high heat. Add chicken and sauté until golden brown on both sides and cooked through. Remove and divide among 4 plates.

Reduce heat to medium-low and stir in artichoke hearts, capers, lemon juice and parsley. Bring to a boil. Whisk in butter quickly, just until melted. Pour sauce over chicken and serve. *Makes 4 servings*

ORANGE–ALMOND CHICKEN

- 6 boneless skinless chicken breasts
- Salt and black pepper
- 1½ cups sliced almonds
- 2 tablespoons flour
- Grated peel of 1 medium orange (about 2 teaspoons)
- 1 egg
- 2 tablespoons water
- 2 to 4 tablespoons olive oil
- Juice of 2 medium oranges (about ½ cup)
- ¾ cup chicken broth
- 1 tablespoon Dijon mustard
- Additional grated orange peel and almonds (optional)

1. Place plastic wrap over chicken breasts and pound to ¼-inch thickness; season with salt and pepper. Place almonds and flour in food processor; process using on/off pulsing action until coarse crumbs form. Add orange peel and pulse to combine.

2. Lightly beat egg and water in shallow bowl. Spread almond mixture on plate. Coat chicken in egg mixture, then in almond mixture, pressing to adhere.

3. Heat 2 tablespoons oil in large skillet over medium-high heat. Cook chicken in batches 10 minutes or until browned and no longer pink in center, turning once. Add additional oil, if necessary. Transfer chicken to plate.

4. Add orange juice to same skillet; cook and stir until reduced by about half, stirring to scrape up browned bits. Add broth and mustard; cook and stir 2 to 3 minutes. Pour over chicken. Garnish with additional orange peel and almonds.

Makes 6 servings

Serving Suggestion: Serve with steamed French-cut green beans.

CORNBREAD CHICKEN POT PIE

- 1 can (10¾ ounces) CAMPBELL'S® Condensed Cream of Chicken Soup (Regular or 98% Fat Free)
- ⅛ teaspoon ground black pepper
- 2 cups cubed cooked chicken
- 1 can (about 8 ounces) whole kernel corn, drained
- 1 package (11 ounces) refrigerated cornbread twists

1. Heat the oven to 425°F.

2. Stir the soup, black pepper, chicken and corn in a 2-quart saucepan over medium heat. Cook and stir until hot and bubbling. Pour the chicken mixture into a 9-inch pie plate.

3. Separate the cornbread into 8 pieces along the perforations. (Do not unroll the dough.) Place over the hot chicken mixture. Bake for 15 minutes or until the bread is golden. *Makes 4 servings*

Prep Time: 10 minutes
Bake Time: 15 minutes

OVEN BARBECUE CHICKEN

- 1 cup barbecue sauce
- ¼ cup honey
- 2 tablespoons soy sauce
- 2 teaspoons grated fresh ginger
- ½ teaspoon dry mustard
- 1 whole chicken, cut up (about 3½ pounds)

Preheat oven to 350°F. Grease shallow baking dish. Combine barbecue sauce, honey, soy sauce, ginger and mustard in small bowl; mix well. Place chicken in prepared baking dish. Brush with sauce mixture. Bake chicken 35 minutes or until cooked through (165°F). *Makes 4 to 6 servings*

Prep Time: 5 minutes
Cook Time: 35 minutes

CHICKEN WITH ITALIAN SAUSAGE

- 10 ounces bulk mild or hot Italian sausage
- 6 boneless skinless chicken thighs
- 1 can (about 15 ounces) white beans, rinsed and drained
- 1 can (about 15 ounces) red beans, rinsed and drained
- 1 cup chicken broth
- 1 medium onion, chopped
- ½ teaspoon salt
- ¼ teaspoon black pepper
- Chopped fresh parsley (optional)

Slow Cooker Directions

1. Brown sausage in large skillet over medium-high heat, stirring to break up meat; drain. Transfer to 4-quart slow cooker.

2. Place chicken, beans, broth, onion, salt and pepper in slow cooker. Cover; cook on LOW 5 to 6 hours.

3. Slice chicken; serve with sausage mixture. Garnish with parsley. *Makes 6 servings*

Prep Time: 15 minutes
Cook Time: 5 to 6 hours

CHICKEN PARMESAN PASTA TOSS

1 jar (1 pound 10 ounces) RAGÚ® Organic Pasta Sauce
1 package (12 ounces) baked breaded chicken breast tenders, heated according to package directions
8 ounces fusilli, bucati or your favorite pasta, cooked and drained
2 cups shredded mozzarella cheese (about 8 ounces)

1. In 2-quart saucepan, heat Pasta Sauce.

2. In large serving bowl, combine hot Sauce, chicken, pasta, and 1 cup cheese. Top with remaining 1 cup cheese and serve immediately. *Makes 4 servings*

Prep Time: 20 minutes

SPICY SHREDDED CHICKEN

6 boneless skinless chicken breasts (about 1½ pounds)
1 jar (16 ounces) salsa
Flour tortillas, warmed

Slow Cooker Directions

Place chicken in slow cooker. Cover with salsa. Cover; cook on LOW 6 to 8 hours or until chicken is tender. Shred chicken with 2 forks; serve with tortillas. *Makes 6 servings*

ITALIAN COUNTRY–STYLE BRAISED CHICKEN

- ½ cup dried porcini mushrooms (about ½ ounce)
- ¼ cup all-purpose flour
- 1 teaspoon salt
- ½ teaspoon black pepper
- 1 whole chicken (3½ to 4 pounds), cut up
- 3 tablespoons olive oil
- 2 ounces bacon or pancetta, chopped
- 1 medium onion, chopped
- 2 carrots, thinly sliced
- 3 cloves garlic, minced
- 1 cup chicken broth
- 1 tablespoon tomato paste
- 1 cup pitted green Italian olives

1. Place mushrooms in small bowl; cover with boiling water. Let stand 15 to 20 minutes or until mushrooms are tender. Strain mushrooms, reserving liquid. Remove and discard stems; chop mushrooms.

2. Combine flour, salt and pepper in large resealable food storage bag. Add 1 or 2 pieces of chicken at a time; toss to coat. Discard any remaining flour mixture.

3. Heat oil in large skillet over medium heat. Brown chicken in batches 15 minutes, turning once. Transfer chicken to plate.

4. Drain all but 1 tablespoon oil from skillet. Add bacon, onion and carrots; cook 5 minutes, stirring occasionally to scrape up browned bits. Add garlic; cook 1 minute. Add mushrooms, reserved liquid, broth and tomato paste; bring to a boil over high heat.

5. Return chicken and any juices to skillet. Reduce heat; simmer 20 minutes or until chicken is cooked through and sauce thickens, turning once. Stir in olives; cook until heated through.

Makes 4 to 6 servings

SWEET & CRISPY OVEN–BAKED CHICKEN

1 pound boneless skinless chicken breast halves
¼ cup *French's®* Honey Mustard
1⅓ cups crushed *French's®* French Fried Onions

1. Coat chicken with mustard. Dip into French Fried Onions. Place into lightly greased baking pan.

2. Bake at 400°F for 20 minutes or until no longer pink in center. *Makes 4 servings*

Prep Time: 5 minutes
Cook Time: 20 minutes

CHICKEN WITH HERB STUFFING

⅓ cup fresh basil
1 package (8 ounces) goat cheese with garlic and herbs
4 boneless skinless chicken breasts
1 to 2 tablespoons olive oil

1. Place basil in food processor; process using on/off pulsing action until chopped. Cut goat cheese into large pieces and add to food processor; process using on/off pulsing action until combined.

2. Preheat oven to 350°F. Place plastic wrap over chicken breasts and pound to ¼-inch thickness.

3. Shape about 2 tablespoons of cheese mixture into log and set in center of each chicken breast. Wrap chicken around filling to enclose completely. Tie securely with kitchen twine.

4. Heat 1 tablespoon oil in large ovenproof skillet and brown chicken on all sides, adding additional oil as needed to prevent sticking. Place skillet in oven and bake 15 minutes or until chicken is cooked through. Cool slightly; remove twine and slice to serve. *Makes 4 servings*

CHICKEN TORTELLINI SOUP

- 6 cups chicken broth
- 1 package (9 ounces) refrigerated cheese and spinach tortellini or three-cheese tortellini
- 1 package (about 6 ounces) refrigerated fully cooked chicken breast strips, cut into bite-size pieces
- 2 cups packed coarsely chopped baby spinach
- 4 to 6 tablespoons grated Parmesan cheese
- 1 tablespoon chopped fresh chives *or* 2 tablespoons sliced green onion

1. Bring broth to a boil in large saucepan over high heat; add tortellini. Reduce heat to medium; cook 5 minutes. Stir in chicken and spinach.

2. Reduce heat to low; cook 3 minutes or until chicken is heated through. Sprinkle with Parmesan cheese and chives.

Makes 4 servings

CHEESY GARLIC CHICKEN

- 4 boneless, skinless chicken breast halves (about $1\frac{1}{4}$ pounds)
- 1 medium tomato, coarsely chopped
- 1 envelope LIPTON® RECIPE SECRETS® Savory Herb with Garlic Soup Mix
- ⅓ cup water
- 1 tablespoon BERTOLLI® Olive Oil
- 1 cup shredded mozzarella cheese (about 4 ounces)
- 1 tablespoon grated Parmesan cheese

1. Preheat oven to 400°F. In 13×9-inch baking dish, arrange chicken; top with tomato.

2. Pour soup mix blended with water and olive oil over chicken.

3. Bake uncovered, 20 minutes. Top with cheeses and bake 5 minutes or until cheese is melted and chicken is thoroughly cooked. Serve, if desired, with crusty Italian bread.

Makes 4 servings

Prep Time: 5 minutes
Cook Time: 25 minutes

• CHICKEN TORTELLINI SOUP •

30–MINUTE PAELLA

- 1 package (about 10 ounces) refrigerated fully cooked chicken breast strips
- 2 tablespoons olive oil
- 1 package (about 10 ounces) chicken-flavored rice and vermicelli mix
- ¼ teaspoon red pepper flakes
- 3½ cups water
- 1 package (8 ounces) medium raw shrimp, peeled
- 1 cup frozen peas
- ¼ cup diced roasted red pepper

Cut chicken strips into bite-size pieces. Heat oil in large skillet over medium heat. Add vermicelli mix and pepper flakes; cook and stir 2 minutes or until vermicelli is golden. Add water, chicken, shrimp, peas, roasted red pepper and seasoning packet; bring to a boil. Reduce heat to low. Cover; cook 12 to 15 minutes or until rice is tender, stirring occasionally. *Makes 6 servings*

CAJUN CHICKEN DRUMS

- 4 chicken drumsticks, skin removed
- ½ to ¾ teaspoon Cajun seasoning
- ½ teaspoon grated lemon peel
- 2 tablespoons fresh lemon juice
- ½ teaspoon hot pepper sauce
- ⅛ teaspoon salt
- 2 tablespoons finely chopped fresh parsley

1. Preheat oven to 400°F. Coat shallow baking dish with nonstick cooking spray. Arrange chicken in dish and sprinkle with seasoning. Cover; bake 25 minutes, turning once.

2. Uncover; cook 10 to 15 minutes or until cooked through (165°F). Add lemon peel, lemon juice, pepper sauce, salt and parsley. Toss to blend, scraping bottom and sides of baking dish. Serve immediately.

Makes 2 servings

LEMON BROCCOLI CHICKEN

- 1 lemon
- 1 tablespoon vegetable oil
- 4 skinless, boneless chicken breast halves
- 1 can (10¾ ounces) CAMPBELL'S® Condensed Cream of Broccoli Soup (Regular or 98% Fat Free)
- ½ cup milk
- ⅛ teaspoon ground black pepper
- Hot cooked rice

1. Cut 4 thin slices of lemon. Squeeze 2 teaspoons juice from the remaining lemon.

2. Heat the oil in a 10-inch skillet over medium-high heat. Add the chicken and cook for 10 minutes or until it's well browned on both sides. Remove the chicken and set aside.

3. Stir the soup, milk, lemon juice and black pepper into the skillet. Heat to a boil. Return the chicken to the skillet and reduce the heat to low. Top the chicken with the lemon slices. Cover and cook for 5 minutes or until the chicken is cooked through. Serve with the rice. *Makes 4 servings*

Easy Substitution Tip: Add whole grains to your diet by serving cooked barley, whole wheat pasta or brown rice instead of white rice.

Prep Time: 5 minutes
Cook Time: 20 minutes

MIDDLE EASTERN CHICKEN

- Nonstick cooking spray
- 1 pound boneless skinless chicken breasts, cut into bite-size pieces
- 1 can (about 14 ounces) diced tomatoes
- 1¼ cups chicken broth
- 2 tablespoons tomato paste
- ¼ package onion soup mix (about 1 tablespoon)
- 1 can (14 ounces) artichoke hearts, drained and quartered
- ¼ cup sliced black olives
- ¼ teaspoon ground allspice
- ¼ teaspoon ground cinnamon

1. Lightly coat large nonstick skillet with cooking spray; heat over medium-high heat. Add chicken; cook 2 minutes or until lightly browned.

2. Stir in tomatoes, broth, tomato paste and soup mix; bring to a boil. Reduce heat to low; simmer 20 minutes. Stir in artichokes, olives, allspice and cinnamon. Simmer 3 minutes or until chicken is cooked through.

Makes 4 servings

15-MINUTE CHICKEN AND BROCCOLI RISOTTO

- 1 tablespoon vegetable oil
- 1 small onion, chopped
- 2 packages (about 9 ounces each) ready-to-serve yellow rice
- 2 cups frozen chopped broccoli
- 1 package (about 6 ounces) refrigerated fully cooked chicken breast strips, cut into bite-size pieces
- ½ cup chicken broth or water

1. Heat oil in large skillet over medium-high heat. Add onion; cook and stir 3 minutes or until translucent.

2. Knead rice in bag. Add rice, broccoli, chicken and broth to skillet. Cover; cook 6 to 8 minutes or until heated through, stirring occasionally.

Makes 4 servings

Serving Suggestion: Top with toasted sliced almonds for a crunchier texture and added flavor.

BBQ CHICKEN STROMBOLI

- 1 package (about 14 ounces) refrigerated pizza dough
- 2 cups shredded cooked chicken
- ⅓ cup barbecue sauce
- 1 cup (4 ounces) shredded Cheddar cheese
- ⅓ cup sliced green onions

1. Preheat oven to 400°F. Lightly spray baking sheet with nonstick cooking spray. Unroll pizza dough on baking sheet; pat into 12×9-inch rectangle.

2. Combine chicken and barbecue sauce in medium bowl until well blended. Spread chicken mixture lengthwise down center of dough, leaving 2½-inch edge on each side. Sprinkle with cheese and green onions. Fold long sides of dough over filling; press edges to seal.

3. Bake 19 to 22 minutes or until golden brown. Let stand 10 minutes before slicing. *Makes 6 servings*

Prep Time: 20 minutes
Cook Time: 19 minutes

QUICK SKILLET CHICKEN & MACARONI PARMESAN

- 1 jar (1 pound 10 ounces) PREGO® Traditional Italian Sauce or PREGO® Organic Tomato & Basil Italian Sauce
- ¼ cup grated Parmesan cheese
- 3 cups cubed cooked chicken
- 1½ cups elbow macaroni, cooked and drained
- 1½ cups shredded part-skim mozzarella cheese (6 ounces)

1. Heat the sauce, 3 tablespoons of the Parmesan cheese, chicken and macaroni in a 10-inch skillet over medium-high heat to a boil. Reduce the heat to medium. Cover and cook for 10 minutes or until the mixture is hot and bubbling, stirring occasionally.

2. Sprinkle with the mozzarella cheese and remaining Parmesan cheese. Let stand for 5 minutes or until the cheese melts. *Makes 6 servings*

Prep Time: 15 minutes
Cook Time: 15 minutes

CRISPY BUTTERMILK FRIED CHICKEN

- 2 cups buttermilk
- 1 tablespoon hot pepper sauce
- 3 pounds bone-in chicken pieces
- 2 cups all-purpose flour
- 2 teaspoons salt
- 2 teaspoons poultry seasoning
- 1 teaspoon garlic salt
- 1 teaspoon paprika
- 1 teaspoon ground red pepper
- 1 teaspoon black pepper
- 1 cup vegetable oil

1. Combine buttermilk and pepper sauce in large resealable food storage bag. Add chicken; turn to coat. Seal bag; refrigerate 2 hours or up to 24 hours.

2. Combine flour, salt, seasoning, garlic salt, paprika, red pepper and black pepper in another large food storage bag; blend well. Working in batches, remove chicken from buttermilk; shake off excess. Add to flour mixture; shake to coat. Place chicken on waxed paper.

3. Heat oil over medium heat in Dutch oven until deep-fry thermometer registers 340°F. Fry chicken in batches 25 to 30 minutes or until golden brown and cooked through (165°F), turning occasionally.

4. Drain on paper towels. Serve immediately.

Makes 4 servings

Note: Carefully monitor the temperature of the oil during cooking. It should not drop below 325°F or go higher than 350°F. The chicken can also be cooked in a deep fryer following the manufacturer's directions. Never leave hot oil unattended.

Prep Time: 15 minutes
Cook Time: 30 minutes

CHICKEN WITH ROASTED GARLIC SAUCE

1 teaspoon olive oil
4 boneless skinless chicken breasts
1 jar (about 28 ounces) roasted garlic pasta sauce
1 cup sliced mushrooms
8 ounces rotini or fusilli pasta, cooked and drained
Grated Parmesan cheese (optional)

1. Heat oil in large skillet over medium heat; lightly brown chicken. Remove from skillet; cool slightly. Cut chicken into thin strips. Return to skillet.

2. Add pasta sauce and mushrooms. Cover; simmer 10 minutes or until chicken is no longer pink in center. Stir in pasta. Sprinkle with cheese, if desired. *Makes 4 servings*

SKILLET CHEESY CHICKEN AND RICE

1 tablespoon vegetable oil
1½ pounds skinless, boneless chicken breast halves (about 4 to 6)
1 can (10¾ ounces) CAMPBELL'S® Condensed Cream of Chicken Soup (Regular or 98% Fat Free)
1½ cups water
¼ teaspoon paprika
¼ teaspoon ground black pepper
2 cups fresh or frozen broccoli flowerets
1½ cups uncooked instant white rice
½ cup shredded Cheddar cheese

1. Heat the oil in a 10-inch skillet over medium-high heat. Add the chicken and cook for 10 minutes or until it's well browned on both sides. Remove the chicken and set aside.

2. Stir in the soup, water, paprika and black pepper. Heat to a boil.

3. Stir in the broccoli and rice. Return the chicken to the skillet and reduce the heat to low. Sprinkle the chicken with additional paprika and black pepper. Top with the cheese. Cover and cook for 5 minutes or until chicken is cooked through and the rice is tender. *Makes 6 servings*

Prep Time: 5 minutes
Cook Time: 20 minutes

BAKED BEAN STEW

1 cup chopped onion
1 cup chopped green pepper
1 tablespoon vegetable oil
12 ounces boneless skinless chicken breasts or tenders, cut into ½-inch pieces
2 cans (15 ounces each) baked beans or pork and beans
1 can (15 ounces) garbanzo beans or black-eyes or 1½ cups cooked dry-packaged garbanzo beans or black-eyes, rinsed, drained
1 can (14½ ounces) diced tomatoes with roasted garlic, undrained
¾ teaspoon dried sage leaves
½ teaspoon ground cumin
Salt and pepper, to taste

1. Cook onion and green pepper in oil in large saucepan over medium heat until tender, 3 to 4 minutes. Add chicken and cook until browned, 3 to 4 minutes.

2. Add beans, tomatoes, and herbs to saucepan; heat to boiling. Reduce heat and simmer, uncovered, 8 to 10 minutes. Season to taste with salt and pepper. *Makes 8 servings*

Tip: Frozen chopped onion and green pepper can be used. Stew can be prepared 1 to 2 days in advance; refrigerate, covered. Stew can also be frozen up to 2 months.

Favorite recipe from American Dry Bean Board

SCALLOPED CHICKEN & PASTA

¼ cup margarine or butter, divided
1 package (6.2 ounces) PASTA RONI® Shells & White Cheddar
2 cups frozen mixed vegetables
⅔ cup milk
2 cups chopped cooked chicken or ham
¼ cup dry bread crumbs

1. Preheat oven to 450°F.

2. In 3-quart saucepan, combine 2¼ cups water and 2 tablespoons margarine. Bring just to a boil. Stir in pasta and frozen vegetables. Reduce heat to medium.

3. Boil, uncovered, stirring frequently, 12 to 14 minutes or until most of water is absorbed. Add Special Seasonings, milk and chicken. Continue cooking 3 minutes.

4. Meanwhile, melt remaining 2 tablespoons margarine in small saucepan; stir in bread crumbs.

5. Transfer pasta mixture to 8- or 9-inch glass baking dish. Sprinkle with bread crumbs. Bake 10 minutes or until bread crumbs are browned and edges are bubbly. *Makes 4 servings*

PISTACHIO CHICKEN

4 boneless skinless chicken breasts
1 tablespoon olive oil
¼ teaspoon paprika
¼ cup finely chopped pistachio nuts
2 tablespoons finely chopped green onion

1. Preheat oven to 375°F. Spray 4 (18×12-inch) pieces of foil with nonstick cooking spray. Place 1 chicken breast on each piece foil. Brush chicken with oil; sprinkle with paprika. Double-fold sides and ends of foil to seal packets, leaving head space for heat circulation. Place packets on baking sheet.

2. Bake 25 minutes. Carefully open end of foil packet to allow steam to escape. Open foil completely; sprinkle chicken with nuts and green onion. Leave foil open and return to oven. Bake 5 minutes or until chicken is no longer pink in center. Transfer contents of packets to serving plates. *Makes 4 servings*

Prep Time: 10 minutes
Cook Time: 40 minutes

CHICKEN COUSCOUS

Nonstick cooking spray
8 ounces boneless skinless chicken breasts, cut into 1-inch cubes
4 medium zucchini, sliced
1 can (about 14 ounces) diced tomatoes
1 can (about 14 ounces) chicken broth
1 teaspoon Italian seasoning
1 cup uncooked whole wheat couscous

1. Spray large deep skillet with cooking spray; heat over medium-high heat. Cook and stir chicken 4 minutes or until lightly browned.

2. Add zucchini, tomatoes, broth and seasoning. Simmer 15 minutes or until zucchini is almost tender, stirring occasionally. Stir couscous into chicken mixture and cover. Turn heat off; let stand 7 to 10 minutes or until liquid is absorbed.

Makes 4 servings

CHICKEN FLORENTINE IN MINUTES

3 cups water
1 cup milk
2 tablespoons butter
2 packages (about 4 ounces each) fettuccine Alfredo or stroganoff pasta mix
4 cups packed coarsely chopped baby spinach
¼ teaspoon black pepper
1 package (about 10 ounces) refrigerated fully cooked chicken breast strips, cut into ½-inch pieces
¼ cup diced roasted red peppers
¼ cup sour cream

1. Bring water, milk and butter to a boil in large saucepan over medium-high heat. Stir in pasta mixes, spinach and black pepper. Reduce heat to medium. Cook and stir 8 minutes or until pasta is tender.

2. Stir in chicken and roasted peppers; cook 2 minutes or until heated through. Stir in sour cream just before serving.

Makes 4 servings

• CHICKEN COUSCOUS •

ASIAN CHICKEN POCKETS

2 teaspoons vegetable oil
1 package (10 ounces) frozen stir-fry vegetables
2 packages (8 ounces each) refrigerated fully cooked chicken strips, diced
1 tablespoon hot Asian chili sauce with garlic (optional)
1 tablespoon hoisin sauce
1 package (about 15 ounces) refrigerated large crescent rolls
3 tablespoons orange marmalade
1 tablespoon plus 1 teaspoon white wine vinegar
1 tablespoon plus 1 teaspoon soy sauce

1. Preheat oven to 350°F.

2. Heat oil in large skillet over medium heat. Add vegetables; cook until liquid has evaporated, stirring frequently. Add chicken, chili sauce, if desired, and hoisin sauce; stir. Remove from heat. Let stand 5 minutes.

3. Separate crescent rolls on lightly floured board. Place ½ cup chicken filling on wide end of each roll; roll up to narrow point. Place rolls, seam side down, on ungreased baking sheet. Bake 18 to 20 minutes or until golden brown.

4. Combine orange marmalade, vinegar and soy sauce in small bowl. Serve with Asian Chicken Pockets.

Makes 6 servings

• ASIAN CHICKEN POCKET •

PECAN 'N' CHEESE–CRUSTED CHICKEN

- ½ cup HELLMANN'S® or BEST FOODS® Real Mayonnaise
- ¼ cup crumbled blue cheese (about 1 ounce)
- ¼ cup chopped toasted pecans
- 4 boneless, skinless chicken breast halves (about 1¼ pounds)
- 4 teaspoons Italian seasoned dry bread crumbs

1. Preheat oven to 425°F.

2. In medium bowl, combine Hellmann's or Best Foods Real Mayonnaise, cheese and pecans. On baking sheet, arrange chicken. Evenly top with mayonnaise mixture, then sprinkle with bread crumbs.

3. Bake 20 minutes or until chicken is thoroughly cooked.

Makes 4 servings

Parmesan 'n' Pine Nut-Crusted Chicken: Use toasted pine nuts and shredded Parmesan cheese instead of pecans and blue cheese.

Prep Time: 10 minutes
Cook Time: 20 minutes

CHICKEN BURRITOS

- 2 cups chicken broth
- 1 cup uncooked white rice
- 1 can (about 15 ounces) black beans, rinsed and drained
- 1 can (about 14 ounces) diced tomatoes
- 1 cup shredded cooked chicken
- 10 (6-inch) flour tortillas, warmed
- Guacamole
- Salsa

1. Combine broth and rice in medium saucepan; bring to a boil over high heat. Reduce heat; simmer 10 minutes or until rice is tender. Add beans, tomatoes and chicken; cook 10 minutes or until mixture is heated through.

2. Divide mixture evenly among tortillas. Serve with guacamole and salsa.

Makes 10 servings

SPICY MESQUITE CHICKEN FETTUCCINE

- 1 tablespoon chili powder
- 1 teaspoon ground cumin
- 1 teaspoon paprika
- ¼ teaspoon ground red pepper
- 8 ounces uncooked fettuccine
- 2 teaspoons vegetable oil
- 1 pound mesquite marinated chicken breasts, cut into bite-size pieces

1. Combine chili powder, cumin, paprika and red pepper in small bowl. Cook pasta according to package directions; drain.

2. Heat oil in large nonstick skillet over medium-high heat. Add chili powder mixture; cook 30 seconds, stirring constantly. Add chicken; cook and stir 5 to 6 minutes or until cooked through. Add pasta to skillet; stir. Cook 1 to 2 minutes or until heated through. *Makes 4 servings*

HONEY–ROASTED CHICKEN AND BUTTERNUT SQUASH

- 1 butternut squash, peeled and cut into chunks (about 1 pound)
- Salt and black pepper
- 6 chicken thighs
- 1 tablespoon honey

1. Preheat oven to 375°F. Spray baking sheet and roasting rack with cooking spray.

2. Spread squash on baking sheet. Season with salt and pepper; toss to coat. Place roasting rack on top of squash; place chicken on rack. Season with salt and pepper.

3. Roast 25 minutes. Carefully lift rack and stir squash; brush honey over chicken pieces. Roast 20 minutes or until squash is tender and chicken is cooked through (165°F). *Makes 4 to 6 servings*

BLACK AND WHITE CHILI

- Nonstick cooking spray
- 1 pound chicken tenders, cut into ¾-inch pieces
- 1 cup chopped onion
- 1 can (about 15 ounces) Great Northern beans, rinsed and drained
- 1 can (about 15 ounces) black beans, rinsed and drained
- 1 can (about 14 ounces) Mexican-style stewed tomatoes
- 2 tablespoons chili powder

Slow Cooker Directions

1. Spray large skillet with cooking spray; heat over medium heat. Add chicken and onion; cook and stir 5 minutes or until chicken is brown.

2. Combine chicken mixture, beans, tomatoes and chili powder in 5-quart slow cooker. Cover; cook on LOW 4 to 4½ hours.

Makes 6 servings

ARROZ CON POLLO

- 6 chicken thighs, skin removed
- 1 can (14½ ounces) chicken broth
- 1 can (14½ ounces) stewed tomatoes
- 1 package (10 ounces) frozen peas
- 1 package (8 ounces) Spanish-style yellow rice mix
- 1½ cups *French's®* French Fried Onions, divided

Slow Cooker Directions

1. Coat slow cooker with vegetable cooking spray. Combine chicken, broth and tomatoes in slow cooker. Cover and cook on LOW setting for 4 to 5 hours (or on HIGH for 2 to 2½ hours) until chicken is fork-tender.

2. Stir in peas and rice mix. Cover and cook on LOW setting for 2 to 3 hours (or on HIGH for 1 to 1½ hours) until rice is cooked and all liquid is absorbed. Stir in ¾ *cup* French Fried Onions. Spoon soup into serving bowls; top with remaining onions.

Makes 6 servings

• BLACK AND WHITE CHILI •

BAKED CHICKEN WITH BACON–TOMATO SAUCE

2 cups fire-roasted diced tomatoes*
6 slices bacon, cut into 1-inch pieces
4 pounds bone-in chicken pieces
¾ teaspoon salt, divided
¼ teaspoon black pepper
Nonstick cooking spray
1 onion, cut into ⅓-inch slices

**Fire-roasted tomatoes give this dish a deeper, more complex flavor. Look for them in your supermarket or specialty store next to the other canned tomato products.*

1. Preheat oven to 450°F. Spread tomatoes on bottom of 13×9-inch baking dish.

2. Cook bacon in large nonstick skillet over medium-high heat until crisp. Transfer to paper towels; drain. Reserve skillet and drippings.

3. Season chicken with ½ teaspoon salt and pepper. Coat another large nonstick skillet with cooking spray; heat over medium-high heat. Add chicken; cook 8 minutes or until browned and crisp, turning once. Transfer to baking dish. Bake 30 to 40 minutes or until chicken is no longer pink in center.

4. Meanwhile, cook onion slices in reserved bacon drippings 8 minutes or until golden, stirring occasionally. Transfer to brown paper bag with slotted spoon. Add remaining ¼ teaspoon salt; shake to degrease onions and mix with salt.

5. Transfer chicken and tomatoes to serving plate; sprinkle with bacon and onions. *Makes 4 servings*

FIERY GRILLED CHICKEN

- ¼ cup olive oil
- 3 tablespoons fresh lemon juice
- 6 cloves garlic, minced
- 1 to 2 teaspoons red pepper flakes
- 8 chicken thighs, skinned (2½ to 3 pounds)
- 3 tablespoons butter, softened
- 1 teaspoon dried rubbed sage
- 1 teaspoon dried thyme
- ¾ teaspoon coarse salt
- ¼ teaspoon ground red pepper or black pepper
- Lemon wedges

1. Combine oil, lemon juice, garlic and pepper flakes in resealable food storage bag. Add chicken. Seal bag; turn to coat. Refrigerate at least 1 hour or up to 8 hours, turning once.

2. Prepare grill for direct cooking. Drain chicken; reserve marinade. Place chicken on grid over medium-high heat; brush with reserved marinade. Grill, covered, 8 minutes. Turn chicken; brush with remaining reserved marinade. Grill, covered, 8 to 10 minutes or until cooked through (165°F).

3. Meanwhile, combine butter, sage, thyme, salt and red pepper in small bowl; mix well. Spread herb butter over chicken just before serving. Serve with lemon wedges. *Makes 4 to 6 servings*

PENNE WITH ROASTED CHICKEN & VEGETABLES

- 1 whole roasted chicken (about 2 pounds)
- 1 box (16 ounces) uncooked penne pasta
- 1 pound roasted vegetables, cut into bite-size pieces
- ⅓ cup shredded Parmesan cheese
- Freshly ground black pepper

1. Remove chicken meat from bones and shred. Discard bones and skin.

2. Cook pasta according to package directions; drain and return to pan. Add chicken and vegetables; toss until heated through. Sprinkle with cheese and season with pepper. *Makes 6 servings*

SAVORY DILL CHICKEN

2 tablespoons BERTOLLI® Olive Oil
1½ pounds boneless, skinless chicken breast halves
1 cup water
1 package KNORR® Vegetable or Spring Vegetable Recipe Mix
¼ teaspoon dried dill weed
½ cup sour cream

• In large skillet, heat BERTOLLI® Olive Oil over medium-high heat and brown chicken, turning occasionally, 5 minutes.

• Stir in water, recipe mix and dill weed. Bring to a boil over high heat. Reduce heat to low and simmer covered, stirring occasionally, 10 minutes or until chicken is thoroughly cooked. Remove chicken to serving platter and keep warm.

• Remove skillet from heat; stir in sour cream. Spoon sauce over chicken and serve, if desired, with noodles.

Makes 4 to 6 servings

Prep Time: 5 minutes
Cook Time: 16 minutes

HOT SWEET MUSTARD CHICKEN

4 cups small pretzel twists
8 boneless skinless chicken thighs (about 2 pounds)
Salt and black pepper
½ cup hot sweet mustard

1. Preheat oven to 350°F. Line baking sheet with foil. Top with roasting rack; coat with nonstick cooking spray.

2. Place pretzels in large resealable food storage bag; seal bag. Crush pretzels with rolling pin or heavy skillet. (Pretzels should yield about 2 cups crumbs.) Place pretzel crumbs in shallow dish.

3. Season chicken with salt and pepper. Generously brush chicken with mustard; coat with pretzel crumbs, pressing to adhere. Place chicken on prepared rack; bake 35 to 40 minutes or until cooked through (165°F).

Makes 4 to 6 servings

The publisher would like to thank the companies and organizations listed below for the use of their recipes and photographs in this publication.

Bays English Muffin Corporation

BelGioioso® Cheese Inc.

Cabot® Creamery Cooperative

California Olive Industry

Campbell Soup Company

Chef Paul Prudhomme's Magic Seasoning Blends®

Delmarva Poultry Industry, Inc.

Del Monte Corporation

Dole Food Company, Inc.

Equal® sweetener

The Golden Grain Company®

The Hershey Company

Holland House®

Hormel Foods, LLC

McIlhenny Company (TABASCO® brand Pepper Sauce)

National Chicken Council / US Poultry & Egg Association

National Onion Association

Newman's Own, Inc.®

Ortega®, A Division of B&G Foods, Inc.

Pacific Northwest Canned Pear Service

Perdue Farms Incorporated

Reckitt Benckiser Inc.

Riviana Foods Inc.

Sun•Maid® Growers of California

TexaSweet Citrus Marketing, Inc.

Unilever

US Dry Bean Council

USA Rice Federation®

Veg•All®

Washington Apple Commission

METRIC CONVERSION CHART

VOLUME MEASUREMENTS (dry)

1/8 teaspoon = 0.5 mL
1/4 teaspoon = 1 mL
1/2 teaspoon = 2 mL
3/4 teaspoon = 4 mL
1 teaspoon = 5 mL
1 tablespoon = 15 mL
2 tablespoons = 30 mL
1/4 cup = 60 mL
1/3 cup = 75 mL
1/2 cup = 125 mL
2/3 cup = 150 mL
3/4 cup = 175 mL
1 cup = 250 mL
2 cups = 1 pint = 500 mL
3 cups = 750 mL
4 cups = 1 quart = 1 L

VOLUME MEASUREMENTS (fluid)

1 fluid ounce (2 tablespoons) = 30 mL
4 fluid ounces (1/2 cup) = 125 mL
8 fluid ounces (1 cup) = 250 mL
12 fluid ounces (1 1/2 cups) = 375 mL
16 fluid ounces (2 cups) = 500 mL

WEIGHTS (mass)

1/2 ounce = 15 g
1 ounce = 30 g
3 ounces = 90 g
4 ounces = 120 g
8 ounces = 225 g
10 ounces = 285 g
12 ounces = 360 g
16 ounces = 1 pound = 450 g

DIMENSIONS

1/16 inch = 2 mm
1/8 inch = 3 mm
1/4 inch = 6 mm
1/2 inch = 1.5 cm
3/4 inch = 2 cm
1 inch = 2.5 cm

OVEN TEMPERATURES

250°F = 120°C
275°F = 140°C
300°F = 150°C
325°F = 160°C
350°F = 180°C
375°F = 190°C
400°F = 200°C
425°F = 220°C
450°F = 230°C

BAKING PAN SIZES

Utensil	Size in Inches/Quarts	Metric Volume	Size in Centimeters
Baking or Cake Pan (square or rectangular)	8×8×2	2 L	20×20×5
	9×9×2	2.5 L	23×23×5
	12×8×2	3 L	30×20×5
	13×9×2	3.5 L	33×23×5
Loaf Pan	8×4×3	1.5 L	20×10×7
	9×5×3	2 L	23×13×7
Round Layer Cake Pan	8×1½	1.2 L	20×4
	9×1½	1.5 L	23×4
Pie Plate	8×1¼	750 mL	20×3
	9×1¼	1 L	23×3
Baking Dish or Casserole	1 quart	1 L	—
	1½ quart	1.5 L	—
	2 quart	2 L	—